THE LITTLE BOOK OF
CHELSEA

A CHELSEA A to Z

Written by Graham Betts and Jules Gammond

THE LITTLE BOOK OF
CHELSEA

This edition first published in the UK in 2007
By Green Umbrella Publishing

© Green Umbrella Publishing 2007

www.greenumbrella.co.uk

Publishers Jules Gammond and Vanessa Gardner

Printed and bound by Butler and Tanner

ISBN: 978-1-905009-24-4

Contents

Abramovich

BORN IN SARATOV, RUSSIA ON 24 October 1966, he took control of Chelsea in 2003 and has since bankrolled their rise up the table. Orphaned at the age of four, Roman was brought up by his paternal uncle and after attending the Industrial

RIGHT Roman's Legionaires

BELOW Abramovich meets the fans in 2003

Institute at Ukhta was drafted into the Soviet Army.

The collapse of communism and the rapid switch to a free economy enabled Roman to acquire vast wealth very quickly as he bought up cheaply shares in the newly-privatised industries and he was soon the major shareholder in Sibneft, the oil company, and RusAl, the aluminum company.

able since then in order that the club can lure the world's top players to Stamford Bridge, together with a charismatic manager to look after the team. Following accusations that his involvement with Chelsea was unpatriotic, he agreed a £30 million sponsorship deal with CSKA Moscow and Sibneft, thus avoiding UEFA regulations that prevent one person owning more than one club.

Whilst Chelsea retained the Premiership title at the end of the 2005-06 season, it is the UEFA Champions League that remains the major priority for the club, prompting Roman to sanction further spending on acquiring the likes of Michael Ballack and Andriy Shevchenko.

By 2005 his wealth was estimated at $13.3 billion, making him the richest Russian in the world and 21st overall.

Although he was known to have looked at a number of football clubs in Europe and was believed to have been a fan of CSKA in Moscow, he invested an initial £150 million to buy the controlling interest in Chelsea in 2003. Almost unlimitless funds have been made avail-

LEFT Chelsea Chairman, Roman Abramovich celebrates winning the Premiership

Armstrong

BORN IN BRADFORD ON 3 JUNE 1924, Ken Armstrong was spotted whilst playing war-time football with Bradford Rovers and the Army. He signed professional forms with Chelsea in December 1946.

He made his debut in August 1947 and would go on to make a then record number of appearances for the club, amassing 362 League appearances and 39 appearances in the FA Cup before moving on in 1956.

A member of the side that won the League title for the first time in 1954-55, Ken also won one cap for England, a figure that might have been considerably higher had he not been susceptible to injuries.

As it was this solid and reliable right half brought his English career to a halt in 1956 and emigrated to New Zealand, turning out for the likes of Easter Union, New Shore United and Gisborne and winning 13 caps for New Zealand!

At the end of his playing career he decided to turn to coaching and died in New Zealand on 13 June 1984.

RIGHT Ken Armstrong shows off his strong arms

Attendances

TOP FIVE

Attendance	Versus	Date	Comments
82,905	Arsenal	12.10.35	Ground record and 2nd highest ever for a League game. Football league
77,952	Swindon Town	13.04.11	FA Cup Round 4
77,696	Blackpool	16.10.48	Football League
76,000 (est)	Tottenham Hotspur	16.10.20	Football League
75,952	Arsenal	09.10.37	Football League

Ballack

BORN IN GORLITZ IN what was then East Germany on September 26, 1976, Michael Ballack is another big name recruit to the Stamford Bridge cause, joining the club in May 2006 on a Bosman free transfer.

He began his professional career with Chemnitzer FC and made his reputation with 1FC Kaiserslautern, earning the first of his sixty caps for Germany in April 1996 and being one of the key players who guided the side to the final of the World Cup in 2002, although Michael had to sit out the final owing to suspension.

Michael joined Bayer Leverkusen shortly after his international debut, costing the club 4.8million Euros, and developed into one of the best attacking midfield players in the world, taking Bayer Leverkusen from mid-table obscurity to challenging for honours – in 2001-02 they finished second in the Bundesliga and runners-up in both the German Cup and UEFA Champions League, although Michael received some compensation by being named German Player of the Year.

That year he joined Bayern Munich for 12.9million Euros and started to collect

his contract expired in 2006 was greeted with jeers by the supporters who once acclaimed him. It was Bayern's inability to do better in the UEFA Champions League that prompted his desire to pursue other avenues, and after expressing his interest in linking up in a midfield that could boast Frank Lampard, he promptly signed for Chelsea in May 2006. Although he helped the club win the Carling Cup and reach the final of the FA Cup, he struggled for form and finished the season early after ankle surgery.

BELOW Captain of Germany Michael Ballack in action for his country.

winners medals, winning the Bundesliga at the end of his first season. He also retained his Player of the Year award and, after a trying 2003-04 season, was back in top form the following term and collected the accolade for a third time – only Franz Beckenbauer with four has won the honour more times.

In four seasons at Bayern Munich Michael helped the club win three domestic doubles, but his announcement that he intended moving on when

Bates

NO FOOTBALL CLUB CHAIRMAN before or since has aroused quite as much argument both for and against as Ken Bates.

Born in London on 4 December 1931, Ken made his fortune from the ready-mix concrete business and dairy farming before he found an interest in football, briefly serving Oldham as chairman during the 1960s and buying a controlling interest in Wigan in 1981.

The following year he bought Chelsea for £1, inheriting substantial debts, a club languishing in the Second Division and a team clearly not good enough to get them out of trouble.

Over the course of the next 20 years Ken rescued the club from bankruptcy, saw off the threat of Marler Estates and turned the ground into one of the best

BELOW Ken Bates generously applauds his team

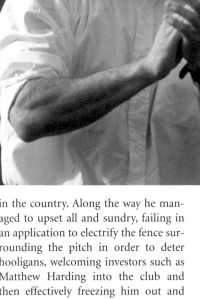

in the country. Along the way he managed to upset all and sundry, failing in an application to electrify the fence surrounding the pitch in order to deter hooligans, welcoming investors such as Matthew Harding into the club and then effectively freezing him out and doing his utmost to deter those he saw as freeloaders.

Aided by massive spending both on and off the pitch Chelsea's fortunes were turned around, with the club enjoying sustained success towards the end of the 1990s and emerging at the start of the new century as a major threat to the previous duopoly of Arsenal and Manchester United. By 2003 debts had spiralled back up to £80 million and Ken accepted an offer of £17 million for his controlling interest from Roman Abramovich, although he remained as chairman until March 2004.

Later the same month he announced his intention of investing in Sheffield Wednesday but this deal fell through and in January 2005 he emerged as the new owner of Leeds United.

Bentley

BORN IN BRISTOL ON 17 MAY 1924, centre-forward Roy remains one of the greatest names in Chelsea's long and illustrious history.

He began his career with Bristol Rovers in 1937 but spent only one year on their books before switching across the city to join rivals Bristol City!

Like many players of his era his best years were undoubtedly lost to the Second World War, but at the end of hostilities he moved north to join Newcastle United in June 1946. He was to make 48 League appearances for the Magpies, scoring 22 goals.

In January 1948 Chelsea paid £11,000 to bring him south and, given that he went on to score 149 goals in 366 appearances in League and cup, it must rank as one of the best deals in the club's history.

A member of the League championship winning side in 1954-55, Roy also netted in the following season's Charity Shield.

His Chelsea career came to an end in August 1956 and once again he moved across a city, this time signing for Fulham (the transfer came to £8,500, meaning Chelsea had paid just £2,500 for eight years use out of Roy, during which he was top scorer in every season!).

By now lacking in pace, Roy managed to score 23 goals in 143 appearances for the Cottagers and finished his playing career with Queens Park Rangers.

He later moved into management, taking charge at Reading and Swansea Town. Roy also proved his worth on the international scene, netting seven goals for England in just 12 appearances.

Blunstone

BORN IN CREWE ON 17 October 1934, Frank joined his local side, Crewe Alexandra straight from school and was thrown almost immediately into the first team in January 1952.

During the course of just 48 appearances for the Railwaymen he was noted as one of the brightest left wing talents in the lower Leagues and numerous clubs sent scouts to have him watched.

In March 1953 he was signed by Chelsea for £7,000 and he soon proved that the step up a grade did not phase him, going on to win the first of his five England caps in November 1954 and helping Chelsea win the League championship at the end of the 1954-55 season.

He remained at Stamford Bridge for the rest of his career, finally retiring in June 1964 having helped the club restore their place in the top flight in 1962-63.

During the course of nearly 350 first team appearances for Chelsea he scored over 50 goals, an adequate return for a winger, but it was the goals he created for the likes of Roy Bentley and then Jimmy Greaves that ensures his place in Chelsea folklore.

ABOVE Frank Blunstone pictured in the 1950s

Bonetti

BORN IN PUTNEY ON THE 27 September 1941, to Swiss parents (hence his surname, which made many believe he was Italian!) Peter Bonetti is truly one of the greats from Chelsea's past.

After a brief spell at Reading as a youngster, Peter joined Chelsea in April 1959 after his mother wrote to the club asking for a trial for 'my boy, who might one day make you a useful goalkeeper.' Mrs Bonetti was a master of understatement, for during the course of near on 20 years, Peter made 600 League appearances and 129 appearances in various cup competitions for the Blues.

Nicknamed The Cat because of his cat-like agility in the penalty area, Peter represented England at Under 23 level before collecting his first full cap against Denmark in 1966 and was a member of the squad for the World Cup that year.

Unfortunately, the continued good form of Gordon Banks prevented Peter from winning more than seven caps for his country, although he did get to represent England in the World Cup, in 1970 in the quarter-final.

A member of the team that won the FA Cup and European Cup Winners' Cup in successive seasons in the 1970s, he finished his career at Stamford Bridge in 1978 and had a brief spell playing in the NASL with St Louis Stars. He later returned to Stamford Bridge as part of the coaching team.

ABOVE RIGHT Peter Bonetti – The Cat

ABOVE Bonetti pictured in 1976

OPPOSITE TOP Stamford's Bridge

OPPOSITE BOTTOM Wayne's whirl

Bridge

BORN IN SOUTHAMPTON ON 5 August 1980, Wayne joined his local club as a trainee and was upgraded to the professional ranks in 1997.

He broke into the first team during the 1998-99 season and quickly established himself a regular feature at left back and over the course of the next five years became one of their most consistent players.

Having represented England at youth and Under-21 level Wayne was handed his first cap in February 2002, although stiff competition from Ashley Cole for the left back role often meant that Wayne's best chance of representing his country would come a little further upfield, in a more midfield role.

After five years at Southampton and with 173 appearances to his name, Wayne was sold to Chelsea in the summer of 2003 (on the same day that Damien Duff arrived) for £7 million with Graeme Le Saux making the move in the opposite direction. Although his first full season at Stamford Bridge saw the club end up empty handed, Wayne made many telling contributions from left back, none more so than the winning goal in the Champions League match against Arsenal.

The following season saw Wayne almost a regular for both club and country until a badly broken ankle suffered at Newcastle in February sadly ended his season. By the time he returned to full fitness he was unable to reclaim his place in the side and went out on loan to Fulham during the 2005-06 season in order to gain valuable first team experience. The arrival of Ashley Cole has further added to the competition for places in his position.

Bumstead

BORN IN ROTHERHITHE ON 27 November 1958, John was first spotted playing schoolboy football in South London and represented both London and Surrey Schools.

Invited along to both Queens Park Rangers and Crystal Palace to train and coveted by both clubs he signed as an apprentice with Chelsea in November 1976 before joining the professional ranks.

RIGHT Bumstead keeps a watchful eye on the ball

BELOW John Bumstead in 1983

He made his League debut for the club against Leeds United in November 1978 and over the course of nearly 15 years, injuries notwithstanding, would go on to make 339 League appearances and a further 70 in major cup competitions. A midfield creator of goals and chances for others rather than a goalscorer himself, John still managed to net 38 goals during his Stamford Bridge career.

A member of the side that won the Second Division championship in 1984 and 1989, John was often the unsung hero and highly regarded by his fellow professionals and teammates.

In July 1991 he was transferred to Charlton Athletic and went on to make 56 appearances for the club before his retirement.

Can we play you
every week?

THIS CRUEL CHANT IS SUNG TO fans of Spurs who have failed to beat the Blues in the league for more than 15 years (32 matches). Their last win at Stamford Bridge was Feb 10th 1990, while their last win in the league at White Hart Lane was even further back on August 22nd 1987.

ABOVE Desailly scores against Tottenham Hotspur, 2001

Date	Where	Result	Occasion	Scorer(s)
22/08/87	*Away*	0 - 1	Division 1	–
02/01/88	Home	0 - 0	Division 1	–
16/09/89	*Away*	4 - 1	Division 1	Dixon, Wilson(2), Clarke
10/02/90	Home	1 - 2	Division 1	Bumstead
01/12/90	Home	3 - 2	Division 1	Dixon, Bumstead, Durie
02/03/91	*Away*	1 - 1	Division 1	Durie
24/08/91	*Away*	3 - 1	Division 1	Dixon, Wilson, Townsend
11/01/92	Home	2 - 0	Division 1	Allen, Wise
15/12/92	*Away*	2 - 1	Premiership	Newton(2)
20/03/93	Home	1 - 1	Premiership	Cascarino
01/09/93	*Away*	1 - 1	Premiership	Cascarino
27/02/94	Home	4 - 3	Premiership	Donaghy, Spencer, Stein(2)

CAN WE PLAY YOU EVERY WEEK

Date	Where	Result	Occasion	Scorer(s)
23/11/94	*Away*	0 - 0	Premiership	
11/02/95	Home	1 - 1	Premiership	Wise
25/11/95	Home	0 - 0	Premiership	
27/04/96	*Away*	1 - 1	Premiership	Hughes
26/10/96	Home	3 - 1	Premiership	Lee, Gullit, Di Matteo
01/02/97	*Away*	2 - 1	Premiership	Di Matteo, o.g.
06/12/98	*Away*	6 - 1	Premiership	Flo(3), Petrescu, Nicholls, Di Matteo
11/04/98	Home	2 - 0	Premiership	Flo, Vialli
19/12/98	Home	2 - 0	Premiership	Poyet, Flo
10/05/99	*Away*	2 - 2	Premiership	Poyet, Goldbaek
12/01/00	Home	1 - 0	Premiership	Weah
05/02/00	*Away*	1 - 0	Premiership	Lambourde
28/10/00	Home	3 - 0	Premiership	Hasselbaink(2), Zola
17/04/01	*Away*	3 - 0	Premiership	Hasselbaink, Poyet, Gudjohnsen
16/09/01	*Away*	3 - 2	Premiership	Hasselbaink (2), Desailly
13/03/02	Home	4 - 0	Premiership	Hasselbaink (3), Lampard
03/11/02	*Away*	0 - 0	Premiership	
01/02/03	Home	1 - 1	Premiership	Zola
13/09/03	Home	4 - 2	Premiership	Lampard, Mutu (2), Hasselbaink
03/04/04	*Away*	1 - 0	Premiership	Hasselbaink
19/09/04	Home	0 - 0	Premiership	
15/01/05	*Away*	2 - 0	Premiership	Lampard (2)
27/08/05	*Away*	2 - 0	Premiership	Del Horno, Duff
11/03/06	Home	1 - 0	Premiership	Makelele

ABOVE RIGHT Frank Lampard scores from the penalty spot, 2005

BELOW Edgar Davids takes on Michael Essien in August 2005

Carvalho

BORN IN AMARANTE, near Porto on 18 May 1978, he made his name with FC Porto, helping the club win successive Portuguese League titles in 2002-03 and 2003-04, the UEFA Cup in 2003 and the Champions League in 2004.

Considered one of the key performers within the Porto side, he was one of the first players Jose Mourinho identified as a necessity for his new-look Chelsea.

There was considerable competition for his signature too, for Porto's surprise victory in the Champions League had the traditional big guns of Europe casting envious eyes at the side.

It cost Chelsea a reported £20 million to bring the top class defender to Stamford Bridge but the partnership he quickly established with John Terry at the heart of the defence meant it was money well spent. At the end of the season he helped Chelsea win the Premiership and League Cup, meaning he won two trophies per season in each of three, having to settle for just the Premiership in 2005-06.

A full Portuguese international, Ricardo was equally important to the national side during their campaign for the 2004 European Championships, finishing runners-up to Greece in the tournament.

LEFT Ricardo Carvalho controls the ball

BELOW Carvalho goes in for a tackle

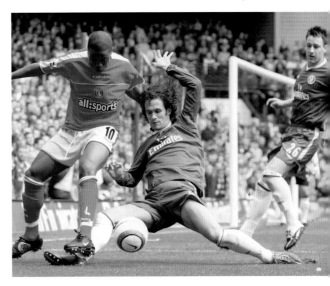

Cech

BORN IN PLZEN IN THE CZECH Republic on 20 May 1982, Petr was seen as something of a surprise acquisition by Chelsea fans, who already believed they had the world's best keeper in Cudicini.

Petr Cech was therefore going have to be something really special; during the course of the 2004-05 season he proved that he was without equal. Petr was just 17 when he made his debut for FK Chmel Blsany in 1999 and less than two years later cost Sparta Prague some £700,000 for his signature.

Four matches into the season he had become a first team regular and set a new national record when he went 855 minutes without conceding a goal, subsequently extending his blank sheet score into the UEFA Champions League. At the end of the season he moved on to France for €5 million to join Stade Rennais and helped the club reach ninth in the League (after being almost perennial

strugglers previously) and reach the semi-finals of the French Cup. In January 2004 he agreed a summer move to Chelsea in a deal that was reported to have cost The Blues £10.3 million, although he arrived amid speculation that his stay might be a short one, since Cudicini was established as first choice and new manager Jose Mourinho had not been responsible for his acquisition. His performances for the Czech Republic during the European Championships, which saw the Czechs' reach the semi-final, meant that there was likely to be a battle royal for the goalkeeper's position at Stamford Bridge.

It soon became apparent that Cech was regarded as the new first choice which was vindicated when he set a new Premiership record of 1025 minutes without conceding a goal (beating the previous record of 694 minutes held by

ABOVE Cech mates

Peter Schmeichel) - a run that had begun in December 2004 when Arsenal scored and lasted until Norwich finally netted.

A sickening clash in a match against Reading during the 2006-07 season left him sidelined with a fractured skull for a considerable spell, during which time Chelsea struggled to maintain their winning ways. When he finally returned to first team duty, he did so wearing a protective cap, but having lost none of his bravery and positional abilities. Time will tell whether the cap stays or goes, Petr Cech meanwhile will continue as the first line of defence for a good few seasons more.

Celery

QUINTESSENTIALLY A LADDISH Chelsea chant which first emerged in the 1980s, based on the more traditional rant " Wem-ber-ley". Fans often throw sticks of celery on to the pitch while singing the chant prompting Man United's Ryan Giggs to observe: "Instead of the usual cups and cans lying around we had sticks of celery. It made me chuckle to think of them popping into greengrocers on their way to Wembley."

BELOW Erm... celery

Centenary 1905-2005

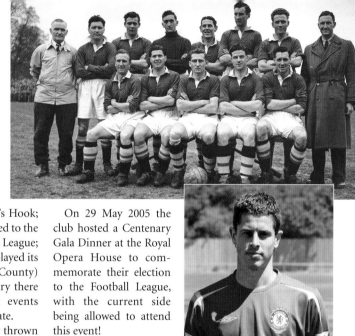

WITH A CHOICE OF THREE dates to chose from (14 March 1905, when the club was founded at The Rising Sun public house, now the Butcher's Hook; 29 May, when the club was elected to the Second Division of the Football League; or 2 September, when the club played its first match away at Stockport County) in which to honour its centenary there were assorted functions and events planned to help the club celebrate.

The first of these was a party thrown at the Butcher's Hook on 14 March 2005, exactly one hundred years since the club was founded at the same venue.

Players from the club's illustrious past, including members of the 1955 championship winning side, the 1970 FA Cup winners and more recent stars joined current manager Jose Mourinho (although none of the current first team squad were permitted to attend as they had an important match the following day!) and other dignitaries in celebrating the first planned event.

On 29 May 2005 the club hosted a Centenary Gala Dinner at the Royal Opera House to commemorate their election to the Football League, with the current side being allowed to attend this event!

Finally, the whole of the 2005-06 season was celebrated as a centenary season, with a special badge appearing on the player's shirts throughout the campaign.

Although the lion is the emblem most closely associated with Chelsea, in light of the creation of Chelsea by Gus Mears and Frederick Parker, perhaps a dog would have been more appropriate in the centenary year!

TOP Football League Champions Chelsea, in 1955

BOTTOM Asier Del Horno displays the 2005-06 centenary shirt

Chelsea ladies

FORMED IN 1992, CHELSEA LADIES FC play at the Belvedere Stadium, home of Hampton & Richmond Borough Football Club.

Within two years the club had won its first honour and they have gone on to win numerous cups and leagues including the Premier League Southern Division title in 2004-05 – mirroring the championship success of their male counterparts!

Chaired by Roman Abramovich and managed by George Michaelas, Chelsea Ladies' success over the 13 years of their existence is perfectly summed up with their theme song – Reach For The Stars by S Club 7!

RIGHT Fulham's Rachel McArthur and Chelsea's Emily Stranghon battle for the ball

Clarke

BORN IN SALTCOATS on 29 August 1963, Steve Clarke arrived at Chelsea a full Scottish international, having won eight caps for his country during his time at St Mirren.

He joined Chelsea in January 1987 and went on to make 330 league appearances for the club, scoring seven goals. A member of the side that won the FA Cup and European Cup Winners' Cup in successive seasons (1996-97 and 1997-98) Steve made more than 400 appearances in total for Chelsea.

At the end of his playing career Steve turned to coaching and was one of Jose Mourinho's first appointments as assistant manager in the summer of 2004.

It was felt that his knowledge of the club and its history, together with the part he had played in shaping it, would be vital to helping Mourinho make an immediate impact at Stamford Bridge. His ability to communicate with the players, especially on occasions when Mourinho was banned from the touchline, were instrumental in helping Chelsea lift the Premiership and League Cup in their centenary season.

ABOVE Assistant manager Steve Clarke

LEFT Skipper Steve Clarke

ABOVE King Cole

Cole

BORN IN ISLINGTON ON 8 November 1981, Joe Cole is another of the graduates of West Ham's ranks that eventually found his way to Chelsea. Something of a child prodigy Joe was courted by many clubs whilst still a schoolboy and eventually signed trainee forms with West Ham United, being upgraded to the professional ranks in 1998.

A member of the side that won the FA Youth Cup (Joe was considered to be the star performer in the side)

he made his West Ham debut in January 1999 and finished the season with eight appearances.

Over the next few years, alongside the likes of Frank Lampard, Glen Johnson and Michael Carrick, Joe developed into one of the best midfield players in the country, usually to be found orchestrating events from central midfield but equally at home on either flank.

The departure of manager Harry Redknapp and assistant Frank Lampard Sr was followed by Frank Lampard Jr's move to Chelsea, and whilst this placed additional responsibility upon young Joe's shoulders, he responded well to the challenge, subsequently earning him a full England call-up.

West Ham's relegation from the Premiership at the end of the 2002-03 season heralded an almost mass exodus from the club, with Chelsea paying £7 million for Joe's signature.

Over the next 18 months or so he struggled to hold down a regular place in the side, which duly affected his England career, but gradually he cut out the sometimes selfish play to work on his all-round contribution and eventually became an integral part of the side that won the FA Premiership and League Cup and retained the League title a year later.

With his club career moving in a positive fashion, his international one is beginning to follow a similar pattern.

ABOVE Joe Cole runs towards the Chelsea fans

Cooke

BORN IN ST MONANCE, FIFE ON 14 October 1942, Charlie began his career north of the border with Aberdeen in 1960 and was transferred to Dundee in December 1964.

His performances for Dundee soon had clubs south of the border taking an interest and in April 1966 Tommy Docherty paid £72,000 to bring him to Chelsea. Although Charlie was bought as a replacement for Terry Venables, his dribbling abilities meant that he was usually employed further out on the right wing than his predecessor.

RIGHT Cooke enters the pitch, 1974

BELOW Charlie Cooke pictured in 1974

After consecutive FA Cup semi-final defeats prior to his arrival, Chelsea finally won in 1967 making the final for the first time since 1915, and Charlie Cooke, the darling of the terraces, was widely recognised as being the reason they made it.

Charlie would have to wait until 1970 before he picked up a winners medal however, but added a European Cup Winners' Cup medal the following year.

After 212 League appearances for the Blues, Charlie moved across London to Crystal Palace in October 1972, but a little over a year later he rejoined Chelsea staying with the club until 1977.

By then he had lifted his total number of League appearances to 299. Having represented Scotland at Under 23 level on four occasions, Charlie won 16 full caps for his country.

Cudicini

BORN IN MILAN ON 6 SEPTEMBER 1973, Carlo followed his father Fabio in signing with AC Milan as a youngster and made two appearances in the Champions League without having made a Serie A appearance.

Unable to break into the first team at Milan he also suffered a succession of injuries, including a wrist injury that kept him out of the game for almost two years. Loan spells at Como and Prato enabled him to at least figure in the League, making a total of 36 appearances for these clubs before a third loan, this time with Lazio, followed in 1996. Unfortunately he again suffered from injuries, restricting him to just a single appearance for Lazio and he was then moved on down the League to Castel Di Sangro.

There his career might have continued towards its conclusion, but Chelsea manager Gianluca Vialli required cover for Ed De Goey and had heard good reports of Carlo, prompting a year loan spell that subsequently became permanent. Age eventually caught up with Ed De Goey and, despite fierce competition from Mark Bosnich, Carlo eventually made the goalkeeping berth his own. He was voted Player of the Year in 2001-02 and quickly established a reputation as one of the best goalkeepers in the Premiership, but further injuries eventually forced Chelsea to look for cover.

BELOW Carlo Cudicini in training

career, a winners medal in the 2005 League cup final, was sadly denied owing to suspension.

An extremely agile goalkeeper, Carlo Cudicini could walk into the first team of virtually every other side in the Premiership; it is unfortunate that the only goalkeeper better than him should play for the same club!

ABOVE Carlo has his hands safely on the ball

RIGHT Cudicini directs his defence

OPPOSITE RIGHT Marcel magic

They eventually found Petr Cech during the summer of 2004 and he was soon given the nod as first choice, leaving Carlo as second choice but used for domestic cup competitions.

What should have been a highlight of Carlo's

Desailly

BORN IN ACCRA, GHANA ON 7 September 1968, Marcel moved to France whilst still a young child when he was adopted by a French diplomat. An early aptitude towards football saw him signed by FC Nantes in 1986.

Six years and 164 League appearances in defence of Nantes later he was signed by Olympique de Marseille and at the end of his first season with the club had helped them win the UEFA Champions League (the first season under its new format) against AC Milan.

Marseille were subsequently stripped of their title, although Marcel's performances had registered with AC Milan, for they signed him midway through the season and he finished 1993-94 helping his new club make up for the previous year's disappointment by winning the UEFA Champions League 4-0 against Barcelona.

his ability he could play equally well in midfield.

The winner of 116 French caps (67 of these were collected whilst he was a Chelsea player, making him the club's most capped player), he collected winners medals in both the World Cup (1998) and European Championships (2000) for his adopted country.

The summer of 2004 saw him draw a close to both his international career and his time at Stamford Bridge, subsequently moving on to Qatar to play for Al Gharafa.

Marcel thus became the first player to collect winners medals in consecutive seasons with different clubs.

After helping AC Milan to two domestic League titles during his time with the club, he left in the summer of 1998 to join Chelsea and added to his medal tally with an FA Cup winners' medal in 2000.

A stylish, unhurried performer, Marcel made 158 appearances for the Blues and was highly regarded by both the fans and his team-mates. Although he began his career in defence, such was

Dixon

BORN IN LUTON ON 24 JULY 1961, Kerry was on the books of Spurs as an apprentice but failed to make the grade at White Hart Lane, subsequently slipping out of League football and joining Dunstable Town.

He netted 52 goals in a year and had League clubs taking an interest again, joining Reading in July 1980 for £20,000 and soon establishing himself as a pro-lific goalscorer. In August 1983 Chelsea paid £175,000 to bring him to Stamford Bridge and he established an understanding with fellow striker David Speedie, netting 28 goals as the club won the Second Division championship in 1983-84.

Kerry continued to score goals in the top flight, finishing his first season as the division's top scorer and prompting calls for an England call-up, which were finally answered when he appeared against Mexico in 1985.

ABOVE Kerry scores again

Kerry continued to score goals for Chelsea until July 1992 when having lost his place to Tony Cascarino, he was sold to Southampton for £575,000, having netted 147 League goals in 335 appearances for The Blues.

His total tally of 193 goals for Chelsea puts him in second place in the list of

RIGHT A youthful Kerry Dixon

BELOW Kerry gold

all time goalscorers for The Blues, just nine behind Bobby Tambling. He didn't settle at The Dell, making just nine appearances and after a spell on loan at Luton made the deal permanent in February 1993.

He later had spells at Millwall, Watford and Doncaster Rovers, where he was briefly player-manager, before returning to the non-League game with Dunstable.

Although his time at Chelsea was barren trophy wise (apart from two Second Division championships), Kerry's goals helped re-establish the club amongst the elite in English football and he won eight caps for England, scoring four goals.

Docherty

BORN IN GLASGOW ON 24 AUGUST 1928, Tommy played just four games for Chelsea but made his name as manager, taking over from Ted Drake in 1962.

A tough-tackling wing half in his playing days, he earned his reputation with Preston North End, joining the club in 1949 from Celtic. The highlight of his career was a runners-up medal in the 1954 FA Cup Final, despite leading at one stage, and after 324 appearances for the Deepdale club, Tommy moved to Arsenal in 1958.

He was with the Gunners for three years, making 83 appearances before his switch to Stamford Bridge in September 1961. Five months later he was appointed manager after Ted Drake's departure, but despite the change Chelsea still ended the season relegated from the First Division.

Tommy Docherty re-organised the club and took them back up at the first

BELOW Tommy Docherty shares a joke during a training session

DOCHERTY

RIGHT Plaster on chin, Tommy Docherty still manages a smile

BELOW Chelsea manager, and proud Scot, Tommy Docherty seems surprisingly pleased that his team are using the coach that carried England to and from matches during their successful World Cup campaign, while Chelsea's Ron Harris looks less sure of its qualities

time of asking and, once returned to the top flight set about turning them into a force to be reckoned with.

He introduced the likes of Terry Venables, Charlie Cooke and Peter Osgood to the side, led them to victory in the 1965 League Cup and stood on the brink of leading them to greatness. Unfortunately Tommy Docherty never got the chance to do so, for he removed from the club those who he felt might undermine his position, including Terry Venables, rowed with the board and managed to lead the club to the 1967 FA Cup Final with most of his players in mutinous mood over bonuses and ticket allocations – they lost to Spurs, with Terry Venables a key component for the opposition.

The ill-feeling generated by the cup run, in particular between Docherty and chairman Charles Pratt simmered on until October 1967 when Docherty resigned.

His managerial career since then, which has taken in the likes of Rotherham, Queens Park Rangers, Manchester United, Derby County and countless others (Docherty claims to have had more clubs than Jack Nicklaus) has been just as turbulent.

Drogba

BORN IN ABIDJAN ON THE IVORY Coast on 11 March 1978 Didier was a late developer as a player but has since emerged as a striker of real quality and potency. He began his career as a right sided defender with Le Mans in the French Second Division and made his debut during the 1998-99 season. It was his conversion to striker that brought a change in his fortunes, being spotted by Division One side Guingamp midway through the 2002-03 season.

The following term he netted a goal every other game to finish with a tally of 17 goals from 34 League appearances and won the Player of the Year award, prompting a £4.1 million transfer to Marseille.

With Marseille competing in European competition on a regular basis the rest of Europe became aware of Didier's abilities and whilst he scored 18 goals domestically in 35 appearances, it was his performances in the UEFA Cup, where Marseille were to finish runners-up in 2003-04, that confirmed his status and knocked both Liverpool and Newcastle United out of the competition.

During the summer of 2004 he was sold to Chelsea for £24.8 million (making him the second most expensive striker in British football history, only

ABOVE Drogba celebrates scoring his second goal for Chelsea in the 2005 FA Community Shield

DROGBA

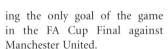

surpassed by the money paid by Man United for Wayne Rooney) with The Blues acquiring a player with explosive speed, immense body strength and an ability to ghost into space whilst losing defenders. Often required to lead the line alone, Didier is the perfect target man, as his 30+ goals during the 2006-07 season would confirm, includ-

ing the only goal of the game in the FA Cup Final against Manchester United.

He was joined at Chelsea by another French import with similar qualities, namely powerhouse midfielder Michael Essien, nicknamed "The Bison", who was signed from Lyon in August 2005 for £24.4 million. Voted Player of the Year in France in 2004, he has quickly proved popular with the fans following his wholehearted displays.

Duff

BORN IN BALLYBODEN, DUBLIN on 2 March 1979, Damien was spotted by Blackburn Rovers whilst playing for Lourdes Celtic and signed with the club in 1995. He made his League debut against Leicester City in the final match of the 1996-97 season and became a regular in the side the following season, making 24 appearances.

He remained at Ewood Park until 2003, making 184 League appearances for Rovers and scoring 27 goals. He cost Chelsea £17 million and looked impressive right from the off until injury interrupted his season.

He finished his first season at Stamford Bridge having made 23 appearances in the League, scoring five goals.

The following year he established a very effective left flank partnership with Arjen Robben as Chelsea won the League and League Cup.

Robben and Joe Cole vied for the flank positions during 2005-06, prompting Damien to move on to Newcastle United in July 2006 for £5 million.

ABOVE LEFT A Duff tackle

ABOVE INSET Damien Duff celebrates scoring against Barcelona

Europe

AFTER COMPETING IN the Fairs Cup during the Sixties, Chelsea entered the European Cup Winners' Cup for the first time in 1970-71 after winning the FA Cup in the previous season.

The competition began with a 6-2 aggregate win over Greek side Aris Salonika in round one and the Blues eventually find themselves back in Greece for the final in Athens after beating Manchester City (2-1) in an all-English semi-final.

Their opponents were Real Madrid, with six European Cups already in their trophy cabinet. The final went to replay after a 1-1 draw with Chelsea hanging on to a 2-1 win with goals from Dempsey and Osgood, to claim their first-ever European trophy.

The European Cup Winners' Cup 1-0 win in 1998 against VfB Stuttgart was achieved with just 20 minutes remaining through a wonder goal from Gianfranco Zola – 30 seconds after he came off the bench. The stunning half-volley strike was the catalyst of the love affair between Zola and Chelsea fans who voted him the club's greatest-ever player.

LEFT Vialli holds the trophy aloft after the 1998 European Cup Winners' Cup Final against VfB Stuttgart

FAR LEFT Chelsea players hold the trophy aloft after the 1998 European Cup Winners' Cup victory

The club has yet to make the final of the UEFA Champions League despite three appearances in the semi-final, which have been lost to Monaco once and Liverpool twice, the most recent being a penalty shoot out defeat at Anfield. But with the Special One in charge most fans and neutrals see it only as a matter of time before Chelsea win the ultimate European domestic trophy.

EUROPEAN RECORD
(up to and including Liverpool (A) - 03/05/05)

Venue	Played	Won	Drawn	Lost	For	Against
Home	61	44	16	3	135	34
Away	64	23	16	25	81	76
Neutral	4	3	1	0	5	2
Total	**129**	**70**	**33**	**28**	**221**	**112**

Famous Fans

FOR YEARS CHELSEA HAVE BEEN associated with a whole range of famous people who have supported the Blues. The height of celebrity fandom came during the 'glory years' around the late sixties and early seventies when the style and glamour of the team was matched by those wandering the Kings Road. Those days have recently returned with Chelsea having the coolest manager and some of the sexiest players on the planet.

POLITICS

Lord Sebastian Coe	Ex-MP/Athlete
Tony Banks	Ex-MP
John Major	Ex-PM
Peter Hain	MP
Peter Bottomley	MP
Ed Vaizey	MP
David Mellor	Ex-MP
Bill Clinton	Ex-President, USA (watched Chelsea in the 60's)

SPORT

Sir Steve Redgrave	Olympic Rower
Jimmy White	Snooker
Tony Drago	Snooker
Sir Clive Woodward	Rugby (England)
Laurence Dallaglio	Rugby (England)
Brian Moore	Rugby (England)
Ian Williams	Rugby (NZ)
Michael Dods	Rugby (Scotland)

Mark Hughes	*Football*
Paul McGrath	*Football*
Paul Merson	*Football*
Mark Wright	*Football*

TV & FILM

Johnny Vaughan	*Presenter, DJ*
Tim Lovejoy	*Soccer AM Presenter*
David Baddiel	*TV Comedian*
Sir Jeremy Isaacs	*Producer/Director*
Chris Barrie	*Actor/Comedian, Red Dwarf*
Lance Percival	*Actor (Carry On films)*
Lord Attenborough	*Film Director (Life President)*
Sir John Mills	*Actor*
Sir Laurence Olivier	*Actor (Died 2005)*
Michael Crawford	*Actor*
Ted Rodgers	*321 Man*
Russell Grant	*Astrologer*
Richard O'Sullivan	*Actor*
Rodney Bewes	*Actor, Likely Lads*
Bill Oddie	*Comedian/TV Presenter*
Gabriel Byrne	*Actor*
Joseph Fiennes	*Actor*
Dennis Waterman	*Actor*
Phil Daniels	*Actor*
Dorian Healy	*Actor*

Shane Warne	*Cricket*
Alec Stewart	*Cricket*
Graham Thorpe	*Cricket*
Chris Cairns	*Cricket*
Chris Cowdrey	*Cricket*
David Smith	*Cricket*
Johnny Herbert	*Motor Racing*
Daley Thompson	*Decathlete*
Eric Bristow	*Darts*
Joe Calzaghe	*Boxing*
Boris Becker	*Tennis*
Pat Cash	*Tennis*
Peter Fleming	*Tennis*
Dick Francis	*Horse Racing*
Clare Balding	*Horse Racing*
William Jarvis	*Horse Racing*
Mark Winstanley	*Horse Racing*

LEFT Boris Becker

BELOW Johnny Vaughan

FAMOUS FANS

Michael Greco	*Actor*
Michael Caine	*Actor*
Bruce Dern	*Actor*
Raquel Welch	*Actress*
Derek Fowlds	*Actor, Heartbeat*
Bill Nighy	*Actor, Love Actually*
Dervla Kirwan	*Actress, BallyKissAngel*
Trevor Eve	*Actor*
David Redfearn	*Magician*
Graham King	*Movie Producer*
Tom Pollock	*Film director*
Charlie Drake	*Comedian*
Huw Higginson	*Actor*
Henry Kelly	*Game Show Host*
Jason Fleming	*Actor (Snatch)*
Georgia Zaris	*'Claudia' in Dream Team*
Guy Ritchie	*Director (& Madonna's husband)*

MUSIC

Bryan Adams	*Musician*
Suggs	*Lead Singer with Madness*
Woody	*Drummer with Madness*
Paul Hardcastle	*'19' Recording Artist*
Madonna	*Singer (her husband's a fan)*
Joe Strummer	*Ex-The Clash*
Paul Cook	*Ex-Sex Pistol*
Steve Jones	*Ex-Sex Pistol*
Morten Harket	*A-Ha Pop Group*
Jimmy Page	*Led Zepplin*
John Taylor	*Duran Duran*
Alan McGee	*Head of Creation Records (Oasis)*
Andy Fletcher	*Depeche Mode*
Dave Gahan	*Depeche Mode*
Lloyd Cole	*Musician*
Nik Kershaw	*80's Pop star*
Busta Rhymes	*US Rap star*
Gary Numan	*80's Popstar*
Andy Cairns	*Lead Singer with Therapy*
Ed Ball	*Musician*
Charlie Harper	*UK Subs*

Alex Paterson	*ORB*
John O'Neill	*Undertones*
Paul Oakenfold	*DJ/Producer*
Trevor Nelson	*DJ, Radio 1*
Graham Dene	*DJ*
Jeff Young	*DJ*
Paul Anderson	*DJ, XFM*
Tim Simenon	*DJ, Producer , Depeche Mode*
Gary Crowley	*DJ*
Gilles Peterson	*DJ*
Iain Baker	*DJ, XFM, ex Jesus Jones*
Damon Albarn	*Lead Singer with Blur & Gorillaz*
Seb Fontaine	*DJ, Radio 1*
Ian Collins	*Talksport radio presenter*
Geri Halliwell	*Singer*

WRITERS/JOURNALISTS

Roddy Doyle	*Playwright*
Andy Hamilton	*Comedy Writer*
Jeremy Vine	*BBC Political correspondant*
Giles Smith	*Sports Writer (Telegraph)*
Nigel Clarke	*Football Writer (Mirror)*
John Motson	*Commentator (can't admit it)*
Martin Tyler	*Commentator (a soft spot at least)*
John Moynihan	*Journalist/Author*
Shelly Webb	*TV Presenter and wife of Neil*
Albert Sewell	*Match of the Day stats man*
Adam Porter	*Journalist - Loaded magazine*

MISCELLANEOUS

Vidal Sassoon	*Hairdresser*
Andrew Dagnall	*Producer*
Stephen Bendall	*Banker*
Martin Greenslade	*Police*
Tim Barnes	*Finance*
Toni Frei	*Travel*
Denis Brennan	*Judge*
Stephen Kelly	*US NASDAQ public company CEO*

BELOW LEFT Blur's Damon Albarn

BELOW Ex-spice girl Geri Halliwell

Ferreira

BORN ON 18 JANUARY 1979 PAULO is another member of the Chelsea squad that was brought in by new manager Jose Mourinho, a long time fan of the full back.

ABOVE RIGHT Paulo Ferreira

ABOVE Ferreira challenges with Craig Bellamy of Newcastle

League titles and the UEFA Cup and Champions League in successive seasons, Paulo joined Chelsea in a deal worth £13.2 million in July 2004. He then went onto help Chelsea complete a double of Premiership and League Cup in 2004-05.

A full international for Portugal, Paulo did not have the best of tournaments during the 2004 European Championships played in his home country, committing a mistake in the first match and being dropped.

A tough-tackling player who seldom suffers from serious injury, Paulo did just that in March 2005 when he sustained a broken foot! Upon returning to first team action he finally broke another unwanted record – he netted his first goal for the club in the FA Cup tie against Colchester United in February 2006

First spotted by Mourinho whilst playing for Vitoria Setubal, Paulo was one of his earliest signings, joining Porto in July 2002.

An important member of the side that won back to back Portuguese

Gallas

BORN IN ASNIERES ON 17 AUGUST 1977, this stylish and pacy defender started his professional career at Caens having graduated from the French football academy at Clairefontaine.

He made 18 appearances for Caens

before being snapped up by Marseille and over the next few years developed into an outstanding defender.

Claudio Ranieri paid £6.2 million in May 2001 to bring him to Chelsea and he quickly established himself within the back four in partnership with first Marcel Desailly and later John Terry.

Such is his flexibility he also played at left back on many occasions including a spell covering for the injured Wayne Bridge. Contract negotiations between him and the club broke down during 2006 and he expressed a wish to play in Italy. The subsequent scandal in that country brought an end to that particular wish, but William was still adamant he wanted to leave the club, finally moving to Arsenal in the same deal that brought Ashley Cole to Stamford Bridge.

ABOVE William Gallas wins the battle of the white boots

LEFT Gallas on the ball

Greatest XI

TO CELEBRATE CHELSEA'S CENTE-
nary, the fans selected their Greatest
Ever XI via a poll on the club's website.
The winners were…

Manager
Jose Mourinho

1	Peter Bonetti
2	Steve Clarke
3	John Terry
4	Marcel Desailly
5	Graham Le Saux
6	Frank Lampard
7	Dennis Wise
8	Charlie Cooke
9	Gianfranco Zola
10	Peter Osgood
11	Bobby Tambling

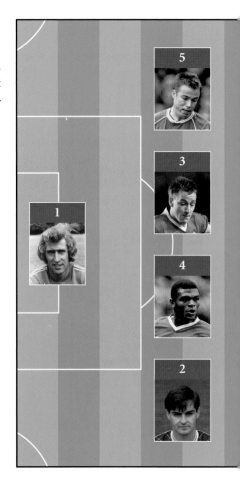

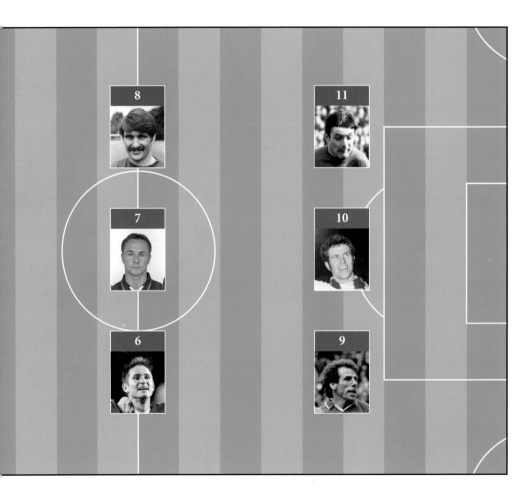

Greaves

BORN IN UPMINSTER ON 20 February 1940, Jimmy was a prolific goalscorer at every level he played; it is no accident that he scored on every major debut he made.

RIGHT AND OPPOSITE RIGHT Jimmy Greaves in training at Stamford Bridge

BELOW A young Jimmy Greaves

Courted by many clubs in his youth and widely expected to join Spurs, Jimmy signed with Chelsea as a junior in 1955 and made his debut for the first team two years later, scoring Chelsea's goal in the 1-1 draw.

By the 1958-59 season he was a regular in the team, netting 32 goals to finish the top goalscorer in the First Division (the first of six occasions Jimmy headed the goalscoring list) and going on to make his England debut (he scored England's goal in the 4-1 defeat by Peru).

In 1960-61 he again topped the goalscoring charts, netting 41 goals and establishing Chelsea's highest number of goals in a season. By then there

were rumblings that Jimmy might be on his way out of the club, for with players still subject to the maximum wage of £20, a few were tempted by moves to Italy where wages were considerably higher. Jimmy signed a deal with AC Milan that was worth £80,000 to Chelsea, although by the time the deal

went through the maximum wage had been lifted and Chelsea and the player unsuccessfully attempted to get the deal cancelled. Never able to settle in Italy, despite scoring on his debut, by December 1961 Chelsea and Spurs were bidding to get him back into English football.

Chelsea would not go above the £80,000 they had received for him, leaving Spurs to clinch his signature for a figure that was reported to be £99,999, or £1 off £100,000 as Spurs' manager Bill Nicholson didn't want him saddled with the tag of being the first player to have cost such a sum.

He needn't have worried, for inside the penalty area nothing phased Jimmy Greaves, as his League record of 357 goals in 514 games and 44 goals for England in 57 appearances would confirm. In March 1970 he moved on to West Ham United where he retired in 1971.

Gudjohnsen

BORN IN REYKJAVIK ON 15 September 1978, he grew up in Belgium, where his father was a player but signed with the Icelandic club Valur when the family returned home following the end of his father's spell in Belgium. Eidur made his debut for Valur at the age of 15 and a year later was snapped up by PSV Eindhoven. Despite considerable competition for places up front at PSV (a club which boasted Ronaldo on its books) Eidur made his League debut for the Dutch club at the age of 17 and shortly after appeared in the Champions League.

A broken ankle sustained in late 1996 effectively brought his PSV career to an end, for he was released and spent the next couple of years trying to prove his fitness with KR Reykjavik.

In 1998 he was 'discovered' a second time, signing for Bolton Wanderers and plying his trade in the Premiership, netting five goals in 14 appearances as the 1998-99 came to a close.

The following season he was something of a revelation, netting 21 goals in the League and various cup competitions, helping the Trotters to the semi-finals of both the FA and League Cups. In the summer of 2000 Chelsea stepped in with the £4 million bid to take him to Stamford Bridge and saw him develop into an excellent striker, netting 40 goals in four seasons and 123 League appearances.

The arrival of Jose Mourinho as manager and the likes of Drogba up front was expected to see Eidur perhaps most at risk in Chelsea's front line, but from his goal on the opening day against Manchester United Eidur proved he was more than up for the challenge.

He ended the season with winners medals from both the Premiership and

League Cup and added a second Premiership medal a year later. That summer he did move on, joining Barcelona for a fee reported to have been 12 million Euros. On 24 April 1996 he and his father created football history during the Icelandic friendly international against Estonia, for during the second half Eidur Gudjohnsen replaced his father Arnor, the first time a father and son had played in the same international match.

Gullit

BORN IN AMSTERDAM ON 1 September 1962, he was brought up in Amsterdam and signed for the local DWS Amsterdam as a schoolboy.

He then switched to Haarlem and developed into an exciting midfield prospect, subsequently being snapped up by Feyenoord in 1982 where he played alongside Johan Cruyff and helped them to the double of League and cup in 1984

In 1985 he moved on to PSV Eindhoven, helping them win the Dutch League in consecutive seasons (1986 and 1987). A £6 million transfer took him to AC Milan in 1987, linking up with fellow countrymen Marco Van Basten and Frank Rijkaard, winning three Serie A titles and the European Cup twice.

In 1993 he moved on to Sampdoria, where he won the Italian Cup, returned briefly to AC Milan and brought to a close his Italian venture with a second stint at Sampdoria.

In 1995 he was one of the key players brought in to Chelsea by Glenn Hoddle and, although not the same as far as pace was concerned, his tactical awareness and ability on the ball made him a star performer.

When Hoddle left to take on the England manager's job Ruud was appointed player-manager, subsequently guiding the club to FA Cup victory in 1997.

Despite this success Ruud was sacked in February 1998 and subsequently resurfaced at Newcastle United. He resigned after five games of the 2000-01 season and had a spell out of the game before becoming coach at Feyenoord in 2004 and resigning again at the end of the season.

A former European Footballer of the Year (in 1987) and World Player of the Year in 1987 and 1989, he helped Holland to their only major tournament triumph, the European Championship in 1988.

ABOVE Chelsea Manager Ruud Gullit holds the FA Cup after the win against Middlesbourgh

Harding

A LIFE-LONG SUPPORTER OF Chelsea, Matthew Harding became more closely involved in the club after answering a call for investors from Ken Bates.

Born on 26 December 1953, Matthew left school with one A level and worked at a couple of banks before landing a job with a new re-insurance company Benfields.

He started as a junior in 1973 and acquired a part of the company in 1980, subsequently acquiring a sizeable share two years later. By the 1990s his share was worth over £150 million and he was a member of the most exclusive of all clubs, the Top 100 Rich List.

In 1994 he agreed to invest some of his sizeable fortune in Chelsea, having been a regular at Stamford Bridge since the age of eight. His investment of some £26.5 million, including £5 million that was spent on the new North Stand, earned him a position of vice-chairman alongside Ken Bates, but the two men were soon involved in a feud, disagreeing over matters such as how the ground should be developed.

Ken Bates, often confrontational, took to banning Matthew Harding from the directors box at Stamford Bridge, with Matthew going off to sit in the North Stand.

Although the pair eventually agreed on a truce, it was always uneasy, but

nothing could prevent Matthew from following his beloved Chelsea.

On 22 October 1996, whilst returning home from a night match at Bolton, the helicopter in which he was a passenger crashed, killing all the occupants. Before his death he had said that his dream was to see players of the calibre of Charlie Cooke and Peter Osgood, winning the FA Cup and Cup Winners Cup in successive seasons back at Stamford Bridge. Two years after his death Chelsea did just that.

ABOVE Matthew Harding waves to fans from his seat in the North Stand

LEFT A tribute in memory of Matthew Harding

ABOVE Chopper and his 1970 troops

BELOW RIGHT Chelsea captain Ron Harris holds aloft the European Cup Winners' Cup after beating Real Madrid 2-1 in a replay

Harris

BORN IN HACKNEY ON 13 November 1944, Ron Harris was the epitome of loyalty to the Chelsea cause. He represented England at both football and cricket at schoolboy level and was captain of the England youth side that won the junior World Cup at Wembley in 1963.

He joined Chelsea as a junior in 1960, following his brother Allan, and signed professional forms in November 1961. Over the next 19 years Ron amassed a total of 655 League appearances for the club, still the record (and only nine of these were as a substitute).

He was appointed captain when Terry Venables moved on and led the club to glory in the FA Cup in 1970 and the European Cup Winners Cup the following year.

Capped four times at Under 23 level, Ron was unfortunate never to have earned a full cap for his country, especially at a time when England needed a midfield destroyer, a role Ron Harris excelled at.

Known affectionately as Chopper on account of the ferocity of his tackles, Ron left Chelsea in May 1980 and wound down his career at Brentford, finally retiring from playing in 1983. He later toured the after dinner speaker circuit, usually in company with former Chelsea player Jimmy Greaves.

Hollins

BORN IN GUILDFORD ON 16 JULY 1946, John gave Chelsea exceptional service over a period of a quarter of a century, twice in spells as a player and once as manager.

Born into a footballing family (his father played for Stoke and Wolves whilst his brother was with Newcastle and Mansfield) he signed professional forms with Chelsea in July 1963 and quickly established himself as the human dynamo of the side with his non-stop running.

John's first spell at Stamford Bridge was to last until June 1975 when he was transferred to Queen's Park Rangers, after 436 League appearances for the club (he scored 47 goals).

John remained at Loftus Road for four years before moving to North London and signing for Arsenal, supposedly in the twilight of his career, but he went on to top the hundred mark for League appearances for the third time (he made 151 appearances for QPR) over the next three years, racking up 127 appearances for the Gunners. Even then John's career was not at an end, for in June 1983, at the age of 37, he returned to Stamford Bridge a second time to finish out his playing days.

BELOW John Hollins about to cross the ball into the box

Had John not left Stamford Bridge in 1975 it is quite conceivable that he would have registered the club's greatest tally of appearances.

Although he won numerous caps at youth, Under 23 and B level, John was unfortunate to have been picked for the full England side on only one occasion, but in so doing he created something of a record that may never be beaten; his brother had previously been capped for Wales!

ABOVE John Hollins (left) in action

RIGHT John Hollins

OPPOSITE RIGHT Alan Hudson chased by another London legend Stan Bowles

After 29 turnouts John finally called it a day and moved into coaching. When John Neal was moved from manager to director in 1985, John stepped into the manager's role and served in that capacity for three years.

Hudson

BORN IN LONDON ON 21 JUNE 1951 (just around the corner from Stamford Bridge), Alan signed schoolboy forms with Chelsea before being taken on as an apprentice in 1966.

Upgraded to the professional ranks in June 1968, he quickly established a reputation as an exciting, flair player and was seemingly on his way to writing a large part in the Chelsea history book for himself.

Troubled by injuries throughout his career, he was forced to sit out as Chelsea won the FA Cup in 1970 but was an integral part of the side that lifted the European Cup Winners' Cup the following season.

His undoubted abilities on the pitch were frequently rocked by revelations and upsets off it and in January 1974 the golden boy of Chelsea was sold to Stoke City for £240,000. His arrival coincided in an upturn in fortunes for the Potteries club, but in December 1976, having fallen out with the manager and with the club in desperate need of money, he was sold back to London, this time to Arsenal, for £180,000.

A runners-up medal in the 1978 FA Cup was the highlight of his brief stay at Highbury and in October 1978 he was on his way again, heading over the Atlantic to join Seattle Sounders for £100,000.

He was to enjoy the less intense atmosphere of North American football for almost five years before returning to Stamford Bridge in

ABOVE RIGHT Alan Hudson celebrates with team-mates after their victory over Real Madrid in the European Cup Winners' Cup Final in Athens

RIGHT Huddy the Hunk

August 1983, but failed to make the first team and moved back to Stoke City.

As club captain Alan made 39 appearances for Stoke during his second spell with the club, finally calling time on his career owing to injury at the age of 34. Whilst fans of Chelsea, Stoke and Arsenal will argue long and hard as to who had the best out of Alan during his club career, there is no doubt he was sadly wasted at international level, collecting only two caps.

His abilities with the ball were unquestioned, but perhaps, like Stan Bowles, Frank Worthington and Tony Currie, doubts about other aspects of his game counted against him when it came to selecting the England side.

Hutchinson

BORN IN DERBY ON 4 AUGUST 1975, Ian Hutchinson's was a career that promised much but fell short of expectations in the final analysis.

He spent a season with Nottingham Forest as an amateur before joining Cambridge United, then a non-League side and was spotted by Chelsea in 1968. He moved to Stamford Bridge in July 1968 and quickly established himself in the first team, but his all-action style frequently saw him sidelined by injuries, some serious, such as a broken leg and nose, others more minor.

He did play an important part in the FA Cup win in 1970, scoring in the first, drawn match with a header (he even out-jumped Jack Charlton!) and firing in one of his speciality long throws from which David Webb scored he winner in the replay.

That was to be the peak of his Chelsea career unfortunately, for continued struggles to overcome a succession of injuries saw him make just 119 League appearances for the Blues before he retired in 1975. Ian died on September 19, 2002 after a lengthy illness.

ABOVE Ian Hutchinson

LEFT Hutchinson launches one of his long throws

Internationals

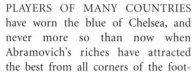

PLAYERS OF MANY COUNTRIES have worn the blue of Chelsea, and never more so than now when Abramovich's riches have attracted the best from all corners of the footballing world.

To illustrate how things have changed, in 1971, Chelsea won the European Cup Winners' Cup with a team of British-born players. They won the same competition in 1998 with just four Englishmen, while today's teams are regularly sent out with even fewer.

Chelsea's most capped player is Marcel Desailly who won 67 of his total 116 caps for France while at Stamford Bridge. For many years it was Ray Wilkins who won 24 of his 84 England caps in blue, but with better players come more caps.

Chelsea's strength in depth is currently such that they can bring on a trio of internationals from the substitutes' bench to turn a game – as they did on the first day of 2005 to secure a crucial single-goal win at Anfield. Joe Cole replaced Damien Duff to score with 10 minutes left, while Didier Drogba took over from Gudjohnsen and Arjen Robben was replaced by Mateja Kezman.

The month of March 2005 saw Chelsea's many internationals hard at work. England's 4-0 victory over Northern Ireland saw Cole and

Lampard on the scoresheet with John Terry his usual rock-like self in a water-tight defence. Damien Duff assisted Morrison's goal for the Republic of Ireland, while Didier Drogba (two) and Geremi (one) scored for their respective countries, Ivory Coast and Cameroon. Other internationals in action that

LEFT Smertin of Russia and Chelsea

BELOW LEFT Geremi of Cameroon and Chelsea

BELOW Huth of Germany and Chelsea

month included Kezman (Serbia), Cech and Jarosik (Czech Republic), Smertin (Russia), Huth (Germany), Gallas (France) and Johnson (England Under-21), plus Carvalho, Ferreira, Morais and Oliveira (Portugal). Unfortunately Robben was injured playing for Holland, a risk internationals and their clubs have to run.

Johnson

BORN IN GREENWICH on 23 August 1984, Glen is another of Chelsea's recruits who began his career at West Ham United.

Signed by the Hammers from school, Glen was promoted to the professional ranks in 2001.

He made just 15 League appearances for the Upton Park outfit and had a spell out on loan at Millwall before moving on to Chelsea, signed by Claudio Ranieri for £6 million in 2003.

Whilst Joe Cole and Frank Lampard were already seasoned and experienced professionals by the time they arrived at Stamford Bridge, the acquisition of Glen Johnson was seen by many as one for the future, although he did manage to make 32 appearances for the club during the 2003-04 season.

The arrival of Paulo Ferreira, further competition for the right full back berth, meant restricted outings during the following season, but time is still on Glen's side. His clashes with his manager, however, which have included forgetting to bring along his passport for a European match in Barcelona and getting caught speeding and shoplifting, have threatened his career, with much of the 2006-07 season being spent on loan at Portsmouth.

His restricted club appearances do not appear to have harmed his international chances, for he was capped by England in November 2003 against Denmark and has since added to his tally of caps.

Jones

LEFT
Vinnie Jones
BELOW Jones pictured
with a large cigar

BORN IN WATFORD ON 5 January 1965, Vinnie spent barely a season at Stamford Bridge but even in that time, in much the same way he had throughout his entire career, managed to make an impression!

He started out his playing career with non-League Wealdstone, combining part-time playing with an almost full time job as a hod carrier.

In November 1986 he was signed by Wimbledon, then enjoying their first season in the top flight of English football. Whilst he was hardly the equal of many of his contemporaries as far as natural ability was concerned, he surpassed them all with regards to his never-say-die and will-to-win attitude was concerned. Indeed, he along with Dennis Wise perhaps best epitomised the Crazy Gang culture that sprung up at Plough Lane and he was an integral part of the side that won the FA Cup in 1988, against all odds, against Liverpool.

In June 1989 he began his nomadic spell, moving on to Leeds United and helping them win promotion to the First Division at the end of his first season with the club. In September 1990 he joined Sheffield United and 11 months later arrived at Stamford Bridge where he linked up once again with Dennis Wise.

Chelsea fans may not have seen the best of Vinnie Jones, but they could not fault his commitment and effort on their behalf. His legacy lives on through the terrace chant Ten Men Went to Mow which he prompted the fans to sing.

A year later he returned to his spiritual home of Wimbledon, even if Plough Lane was but a distant memory, and spent a further five and a half years nurturing a new Crazy Gang.

He finished his playing career at Queens Park Rangers before moving in to the world of acting.

Kit

THE CLUB'S NEW CENTENARY home kit was unveiled in the summer of 2005 prominently featuring the name of the official sponsor 'Samsung mobile' and carrying a number of features that set it apart from any strip that had gone before including a Centenary crest and gold detailing complimenting the traditional royal blue colouring.

ABOVE RIGHT Petr Cech with his new goalkeeper's kit

RIGHT Joe Cole, Asier Del Horno and Damien Duff display Chelsea's new Centenary kit

Lampard

BORN IN ROMFORD ON 20 JUNE 1978 he joined West Ham United straight from school and gradually rose through the ranks.

That he should have joined West Ham was no surprise; his father, Frank Sr was a former player and assistant manager, whilst his uncle Harry Redknapp was manager.

He signed professional forms with West Ham in 1994 but had to wait until the 1995-96 season before making his League debut. He also had a spell on loan at Swansea City before becoming a regular fixture of the West Ham midfield.

His club performances were rewarded with his first full England cap (he had previously represented his country at youth, Under-21 and B level) in October 1999 against Belgium. Everything seemed set for a comfortable career at Upton Park, but the news that the club had sold Rio Ferdinand to Leeds United for £17 million in November 2000 started a period of unrest at the club, culminating in the sacking of Harry Redknapp and subsequent departure of Frank Lampard Sr in May 2001.

Announcing he would never play for West Ham again prompted a number of clubs to make enquiries for Frank Jr and he was subsequently snapped up by Chelsea for £11.5 million.

ABOVE Super Frank!

ABOVE 'Rock-a-bye-baby'. Frank celebrates scoring against West Brom and the birth of his first child

RIGHT Master and Commander

Although he initially struggled to fit into the side he eventually won over the fans with his powerhouse displays and consistency; he has broken both Chelsea's consecutive Premiership and League appearance records, overtaking John Hollins record of 135 games.

His outstanding midfield displays for the Blues won him Chelsea Player of the Year in 2004 and nomination for FIFA's World Player of the Year and the FWA Player of the Year award in 2005. Further club and family milestones arrived for "Super Frank" when he scored his 50th goal for the Blues on his 150th Premiership appearance – just three days after his first child, daughter Luna was born. A second child is due to be born in June 2007.

Le Saux

BORN ON THE ISLAND OF Jersey on 17 October 1968, Graeme began his career at Chelsea in 1987 and spent six seasons at Stamford Bridge during his first spell with the club, making 110 League appearances.

The closest he came to establishing himself as a first team regular came during the 1991-92 season when he made 40 League appearances, but in 1993 he moved to Blackburn Rovers.

A member of the side that finished runners up and then Champions in the Premiership in 1993-94 and 1994-95, he is perhaps best remembered from his time at Ewood Park for a mid-match altercation with team-mate David Batty. He returned to Chelsea in 1997 and was a member of the side that won the League Cup in 1998, although injuries, particularly during the 1999-2000 season prevented him from adding to his medal tally.

In the summer of 2003, having increased his Chelsea League tally of appearances to 230, he moved to Southampton as part of the £7 million deal that brought Wayne Bridge to Stamford Bridge.

It was somewhat ironic that the player who had often replaced Graeme in the England side should now do so at club level, but Graeme did have 36 caps to his name.

At the end of the 2004-05 season, with Southampton having suffered relegation from the Premiership, he announced his retirement from playing and was expected to increase his work as a television pundit.

League Positions

Season Ending	Division	Position	P	W	D	L	F	A	Points
1906	2	3rd	38	22	9	7	90	37	53
1907	2	2nd	38	26	5	7	80	34	57
1908	1	13th	38	14	8	16	53	62	36
1909	1	11th	38	14	9	15	56	61	37
1910	1	19th	38	11	7	20	47	70	29
1911	2	3rd	38	20	9	9	71	35	49
1912	2	2nd	38	24	6	8	74	34	54
1913	1	18th	38	11	6	21	51	73	28
1914	1	8th	38	16	7	15	46	55	39
1915	1	19th	38	8	13	17	51	65	29
1920	1	3rd	42	22	5	15	56	51	49
1921	1	18th	42	13	13	16	48	58	39
1922	1	9th	42	17	12	13	40	43	46
1923	1	19th	42	9	18	15	45	53	36
1924	1	21st	42	9	14	19	31	53	32
1925	2	5th	42	16	15	11	51	37	47
1926	2	3rd	42	19	14	9	76	49	52
1927	2	4th	42	20	12	10	62	52	52
1928	2	3rd	42	23	8	11	75	45	54
1929	2	9th	42	17	10	15	64	65	44
1930	2	2nd	42	22	11	9	74	46	55
1931	1	12th	42	15	10	17	64	67	40
1932	1	12th	42	16	8	18	69	73	40
1933	1	12th	42	14	7	21	63	73	35
1934	1	19th	42	14	8	20	67	69	36
1935	1	12th	42	16	9	17	73	82	41
1936	1	8th	42	15	13	14	65	72	43
1937	1	13th	42	14	13	15	52	55	41
1938	1	10th	42	14	13	15	65	65	41

Season Ending	Division	Position	P	W	D	L	F	A	Points
1939	1	20th	42	12	9	21	64	80	33
1940	1	12th	3	1	1	1	4	4	3
1947	1	15th	42	16	7	19	69	84	39
1948	1	18th	42	14	9	19	53	71	37
1949	1	13th	42	12	14	16	69	68	38
1950	1	13th	42	12	16	14	58	65	40
1951	1	20th	42	12	8	22	53	65	32
1952	1	19th	42	14	8	20	52	72	36
1953	1	19th	42	12	11	19	56	66	35
1954	1	8th	42	16	12	14	74	68	44
1955	1	1st	42	20	12	10	81	57	52
1956	1	16th	42	14	11	17	64	77	39
1957	1	13th	42	13	13	16	73	73	39
1958	1	11th	42	15	12	15	83	79	42
1959	1	14th	42	18	4	20	77	98	40
1960	1	18th	42	14	9	19	76	91	37
1961	1	12th	42	15	7	20	98	100	37
1962	1	22nd	42	9	10	23	63	94	28
1963	2	2nd	42	24	4	14	81	42	52
1964	1	5th	42	20	10	12	72	56	50
1965	1	3rd	42	24	8	10	89	54	56
1966	1	5th	42	22	7	13	65	53	51
1967	1	9th	42	15	14	13	67	62	44
1968	1	6th	42	18	12	12	62	68	48
1969	1	5th	42	20	10	12	73	53	50
1970	1	3rd	42	21	13	8	70	50	55
1971	1	6th	42	18	15	9	52	42	51
1972	1	7th	42	18	12	12	58	49	48
1973	1	12th	42	13	14	15	49	51	40
1974	1	17th	42	12	13	17	56	60	37
1975	1	21st	42	9	15	18	42	72	33
1976	2	11th	42	12	16	14	53	54	40

BELOW Young Chelsea supporters

LEAGUE POSITIONS

Season Ending	Division	Position	P	W	D	L	F	A	Points
1977	2	2nd	42	21	13	8	73	53	55
1978	1	16th	42	11	14	17	46	69	36
1979	1	22nd	42	5	10	27	44	92	20
1980	2	4th	42	23	7	12	66	52	53
1981	2	12th	42	14	12	16	46	41	40
1982	2	12th	42	15	12	15	60	60	57
1983	2	18th	42	11	14	17	51	61	47
1984	2	1st	42	25	13	4	80	40	88
1985	1	6th	42	18	12	12	63	48	66
1986	1	6th	42	20	11	11	57	56	71
1987	1	14th	42	13	13	16	53	64	52
1988	1	18th	40	9	15	16	50	68	42
1989	2	1st	46	29	12	5	96	50	99
1990	1	5th	38	16	12	10	58	50	60
1991	1	11th	38	13	10	15	58	69	49
1992	1	14th	42	13	14	15	50	60	53
1993	Prem	11th	42	14	14	14	51	54	56
1994	Prem	14th	42	13	12	17	49	53	51
1995	Prem	11th	42	13	15	14	50	55	54
1996	Prem	11th	38	12	14	12	46	44	50
1997	Prem	6th	38	16	11	11	58	55	59
1998	Prem	4th	38	20	3	15	71	43	63
1999	Prem	3rd	38	20	15	3	57	30	75
2000	Prem	5th	38	18	11	9	53	34	65
2001	Prem	6th	38	17	10	11	68	45	61
2002	Prem	6th	38	17	13	8	66	38	64
2003	Prem	4th	38	19	10	9	67	38	67
2004	Prem	2nd	38	24	7	7	67	30	79
2005	Prem	1st	38	29	8	1	72	15	95
2006	Prem	1st	38	29	4	5	72	22	91
2007	Prem	2nd	38	24	11	3	64	24	83

Makelele

BORN IN KINSHASA ON 18 February 1973, Claude began his career with Brest before switching to Nantes in 1992. Over the course of the next five seasons he enjoyed considerable

success, helping Nantes to the French title and reach the Champions League semi-finals.

In 1997, having made 169 appearances for the club and scoring nine goals, the defensive midfielder was sold to rivals Marseille. Claude made just 33 appearances for Marseille before moving to Spain and joining Celta Vigo in 1998, re-establishing his reputation and earning a subsequent move to Real Madrid in 2000.

A member of the side that won the Spanish League and Champions League in 2002, Claude enjoyed three successful seasons in Madrid before a £16.6 million transfer brought him to Chelsea in 2003.

He soon became a regular within the side and at the end of the 2004-05 season had won a League championship medal in a third country. He scored his first-ever goal for Chelsea with a penalty in the last minute of the last home game of the season against Charlton.

A French international with over 30 caps to his extensive experience, especially of the Champions League, has been invaluable and he has been a perfect foil for Frank Lampard who likes to get forward while Claude stays back.

LEFT After you Claude!
BELOW Hey Makelele!

Managers

Manager	Year	Manager	Year
John Robertson	1905 to 1906	Geoff Hurst	1979 to 1981
David Calderhead	1907 to 1933	John Neal	1981 to 1985
T Leslie Knighton	1933 to 1939	John Hollins	1985 to 1988
William Birrell	1939 to 1952	Bobby Campbell	1988 to 1992
Ted Drake	1952 to 1961	Ian Porterfield	1992 to 1993
Tommy Docherty	1962 to 1967	David Webb	1993 to 1993
Dave Sexton	1967 to 1974	Glenn Hoddle	1993 to 1996
Ron Stuart	1974 to 1975	Ruud Gullit	1996 to 1998
Eddie McCreadie	1975 to 1977	Gianluca Vialli	1998 to 2000
Ken Shellito	1977 to 1978	Claudio Ranieri	2000 to 2004
Danny Blanchflower	1978 to 1979	Jose Mourinho	2004 - present

McCreadie

BORN IN GLASGOW ON 15 April 1940, Eddie gave exceptional service to Chelsea for many years, both as a player and later as manager.

Signed by Tommy Docherty from East Stirling in April 1962 for a paltry £5,000, he quickly established himself as the first choice left back, injuries permitting.

Over the course of the next 11 years Eddie made 331 League appearances for the club, adding a further 79 appearances in major cup competitions, netting four League goals.

It was his ability to help keep goals out, however, that earned Eddie his place in Chelsea folklore, helping the club win the League Cup in 1965, the FA Cup in 1970 and the European Cup Winners' Cup a year later.

He was equally revered in Scotland, winning a total of 23 caps for his country, including the infamous 3-2 win over then World champions England in 1967.

Eddie took over from Ron Stuart as Chelsea manager in 1975 when Stuart

moved up to General Manager and remained in charge for two years. During his second year in charge Chelsea won promotion back into the First Division and Eddie, a firm favourite of the fans, seemed set to guide the club back to the glory days. Unfortunately the euphoria surrounding promotion had barely had time to settle when Eddie left the club, resigning on 1 July 1977 over unacceptable terms offered by the board to continue as manager.

He was replaced almost immediately by Ken Shellito. Given the up and down existence Chelsea then endured for the next few years, it will always remain an unanswered question as to what Chelsea might have achieved under Eddie McCreadie?

LEFT Eddie McCreadie
BELOW McCreadie gets the better of Leeds

Mourinho

BORN IN SETUBAL, PORTUGAL ON 26 January 1963, Jose Mario dos Santos Mourinho Felix, to give him his full name, is one of only a handful of managers to have achieved greatness without having excelled as a player.

His father was a professional goalkeeper, but despite having spells with minor League clubs, Jose made more of a mark on the management and coaching side of the game, producing dossiers and match reports from which his father's teams benefited.

A degree in sports coaching was followed by a spell as a high school coach and finally a move into higher level football with Vitoria Setubal during the early 1990s.

He then linked up with English coach Bobby Robson when he was appointed coach at Sporting Lisbon, becoming his translator (which earned him the nickname Tradulator, although technically he was employed as an interpreter).

He followed Robson to both FC Porto and then to Spain with Barcelona, where he learned the Catalan language. When Robson returned to PSV Eindhoven, Mourinho remained at Barcelona and worked alongside Louis Van Gaal.

It soon became apparent that having to translate and interpret instructions from learned football coaches such as Robson and Van Gaal had awoken coaching abilities in Mourinho, and

RIGHT Mourinho deep in thought at a press conference

BORN IN GLASGOW ON 6 September 1963, Pat remains one of the most exciting players to have pulled on the blue shirt of Chelsea, irrespective of the talents that are currently being lured to Stamford Bridge. Spotted by Clyde playing minor League football in 1981, his performances in the less frenetic Scottish League soon had scouts from south of the border tracking his progress and in July 1983 he was sold to Chelsea.

His impact at Stamford Bridge was immediate, making 38 appearances and scoring four goals in Chelsea's Second Division Championship winning season, earning himself the

supporters' 'Player of the Year' award (he would repeat the success in 1987) as well as the accolade of the 'most out-standing player in the Second Division.'

He excelled at the higher level as well, helping Chelsea establish their creden-

MOURINHO

President announced he had another coach to take over.

A brief spell at Uniao de Leiria was followed by his appointment as coach at FC Porto in January 2002.

Although the club was languishing in mid-table, was out of contention for the League and faced an uphill struggle to

after expanding his role at Barcelona to such an extent he was contributing to coaching and tactic sessions, he was soon looking for a position of his own. It came in 2000 when he was offered the chance of replacing Jupp Heynckes at Benfica, but after just nine games in charge he resigned when the in-coming

BELOW Jose Mourinho poses with his children Zuca (L) and Matilde (R) and the Premiership Trophy

CFC

Nevi

They repeated their Super Liga success in 2003-04 (albeit with a reduced eight point advantage) and narrowly missed out on the Portuguese Cup, beaten by Benfica for once.

However, there was plenty of compensation to be found in Europe, winning the UEFA Champions League 3-0 against Monaco having previously seen off the likes of Manchester United. Despite or perhaps because of this European success, Jose was soon being courted by most of Europe's top sides and eventually settled on a move to Chelsea, taking over the reins in June 2004.

Although he inherited a top class side from Claudio Ranieri, Jose soon identified areas for improvement and brought in almost a new backroom staff and set about turning Ranieri's nearly men into champions.

He collected his first trophy by beating Liverpool in the League Cup in March and guided Chelsea to their first League title in 50 years at the end of his first season in charge and adding a second League title twelve months later.

Only the UEFA Champions League appeared to blot his copybook, beaten in

ABOVE Mourinho receives a warm welcome in South Korea

even qualify for Europe, Mourinho was confident of his own abilities, promising he would make them League champions the following season.

His impact was immediate, for at the end of the 2001-02 he had lifted them to third place in the table and qualification for the UEFA Cup.

The 2002-03 season saw the realisation of his promise, for they won the Portuguese League (the Super Liga) by eleven points from Benfica, had won the Portuguese Cup (beating another former club Leiria in the final) and had won the UEFA Cup for good measure, beating Celtic in that final.

President announced he had another coach to take over.

A brief spell at Uniao de Leiria was followed by his appointment as coach at FC Porto in January 2002.

Although the club was languishing in mid-table, was out of contention for the League and faced an uphill struggle to

after expanding his role at Barcelona to such an extent he was contributing to coaching and tactic sessions, he was soon looking for a position of his own. It came in 2000 when he was offered the chance of replacing Jupp Heynckes at Benfica, but after just nine games in charge he resigned when the in-coming

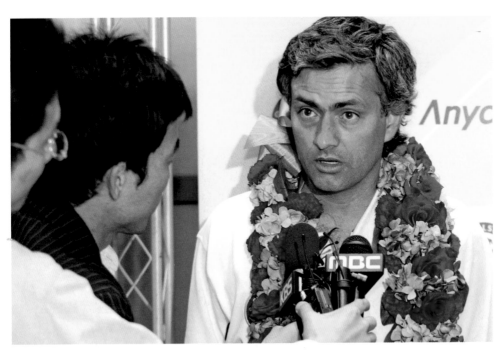

even qualify for Europe, Mourinho was confident of his own abilities, promising he would make them League champions the following season.

His impact was immediate, for at the end of the 2001-02 he had lifted them to third place in the table and qualification for the UEFA Cup.

The 2002-03 season saw the realisation of his promise, for they won the Portuguese League (the Super Liga) by eleven points from Benfica, had won the Portuguese Cup (beating another former club Leiria in the final) and had won the UEFA Cup for good measure, beating Celtic in that final.

They repeated their Super Liga success in 2003-04 (albeit with a reduced eight point advantage) and narrowly missed out on the Portuguese Cup, beaten by Benfica for once.

However, there was plenty of compensation to be found in Europe, winning the UEFA Champions League 3-0 against Monaco having previously seen off the likes of Manchester United. Despite or perhaps because of this European success, Jose was soon being courted by most of Europe's top sides and eventually settled on a move to Chelsea, taking over the reins in June 2004.

Although he inherited a top class side from Claudio Ranieri, Jose soon identified areas for improvement and brought in almost a new backroom staff and set about turning Ranieri's nearly men into champions.

He collected his first trophy by beating Liverpool in the League Cup in March and guided Chelsea to their first League title in 50 years at the end of his first season in charge and adding a second League title twelve months later.

Only the UEFA Champions League appeared to blot his copybook, beaten in

ABOVE Jose Mourinho

the semi-final by eventual winners Liverpool, whilst a year later Barcelona ended their interest in the quarter-finals.

His unbending belief in his own abilities (he refers to himself as 'The Chosen One') is shared not only by Chelsea's fans and players but also, somewhat surprisingly, by many of his contemporaries in the game, including Sir Alex Ferguson!

Nevin

BORN IN GLASGOW ON 6 September 1963, Pat remains one of the most exciting players to have pulled on the blue shirt of Chelsea, irrespective of the talents that are currently being lured to Stamford Bridge. Spotted by Clyde playing minor League football in 1981, his performances in the less frenetic Scottish League soon had scouts from south of the border tracking his progress and in July 1983 he was sold to Chelsea.

His impact at Stamford Bridge was immediate, making 38 appearances and scoring four goals in Chelsea's Second Division Championship winning season, earning himself the

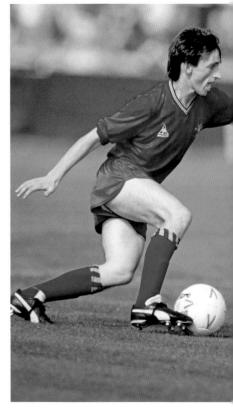

supporters' 'Player of the Year' award (he would repeat the success in 1987) as well as the accolade of the 'most outstanding player in the Second Division.'

He excelled at the higher level as well, helping Chelsea establish their creden-

tials in the First Division and collecting the first of his 28 caps for Scotland.

In July 1988, after five years and 193 League appearances with Chelsea, he was surprisingly sold to Everton and proved as firm a fans' favourite at Goodison Park as he had at Stamford Bridge.

He was to enjoy three and a half years at Everton, making 109 appearances before being loaned to Tranmere Rovers. The move to Prenton Park became permanent in August 1992 and he would go on to rack up just over 200 League appearances for Tranmere before moving back north of the border and turning out for a variety of clubs.

Pat was almost unique among professional footballers during the 1980s, for whilst most of his contemporaries would cite the likes of Phil Collins and Lionel Richie as their favourite musicians, Pat's invariably came straight from the pages of New Musical Express and he was often a guest reviewer for the magazine.

He was equally up to date with political matters; he may have played on the right wing but his politics came from the left!

LEFT Pat Nevin

Osgood

BORN IN WINDSOR ON 20 February 1947 Peter Osgood is one of the greatest goalscorers in Chelsea's history, having netted well over 100 goals during his two spells with the club.

Initially signed as a junior Peter was upgraded to the professional ranks in September 1964 and made his debut the same season, scoring twice in a League Cup tie as Chelsea progressed to win the tournament. Initially seen as the ideal cover for Barry Bridges, Peter made a proper breakthrough during the 1965-66 season until a broken leg brought his career to a temporary halt.

He recovered and emerged to lead the line in his own right, scoring in every round as Chelsea won the FA Cup in 1970, one of only nine men to have achieved the feat.

He netted in both the final and replay of the European Cup Winners Cup the

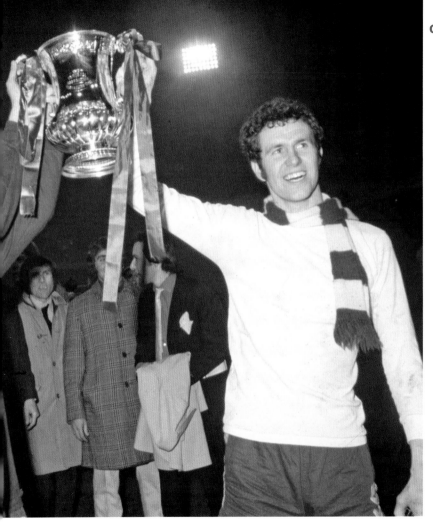

LEFT Ron Harris (left) and Peter Osgood lift the FA Cup after beating Leeds United 2-1 in the FA Cup Final replay at Old Trafford

following season, enabling Chelsea to add a further trophy to their record. For good measure, Peter scored in a final for the third consecutive season in 1971-72, but this time Chelsea lost the League Cup 2-1 to Stoke City.

Peter remained at Stamford Bridge until March 1974 when he moved on to Southampton, having made 279 League appearances for the Blues and scored 103 goals.

RIGHT Peter Osgood
BELOW I want to be os good as you

He remained at The Dell until 1977, apart from a brief period on loan to Norwich City, and left the club with another FA Cup winners medal in his pocket after Southampton had surprisingly beaten Manchester United in 1976.

After a brief spell in America with Philadelphia Peter returned to Stamford Bridge to finish his playing career, registering a further ten appearances and two goals.

A member of the England 1970 World Cup squad Peter won four full caps having already represented the country at youth and Under-23 level. He later worked at Stamford Bridge as one of the greeting legends at home matches and collapsed and died at a family funeral on March 1, 2006.

Pates

BORN IN CARSHALTON ON 10 August 1961, Colin signed apprentice forms with Chelsea straight from school and was upgraded to the professional ranks in July 1979.

He made his debut soon after, appearing in the Second Division match against Orient in November 1979 and over the next nine years would go on to make a total of 281 League appearances for the club, along with more than 50 in various cup competitions. Such was the consistency and reliability of Colin at the heart of Chelsea's defence, only one of his League appearances was as a substitute, an astonishing figure for a man often at the heart of the action.

A member of the side that won the Second Division championship in 1984, the closest he came to a major honour was a winners medal in the much maligned Full Members Cup in 1986,

but as the final was played at Wembley, there is no doubt that the occasion is still warmly remembered in the Pates household.

In October 1988 he was sold to Charlton Athletic, going on to make 38 appearances for the club (again with only one substitute's appearance) before moving to North London and Arsenal. Used more sparingly at Highbury than previously in his career,

ABOVE Colin Pates

Colin's final tally of 21 appearances included nine as substitute, and in March 1991 he was sent on loan to Brighton & Hove Albion for 17 appearances.

His move to the south coast became permanent in August 1993 and he finished his career with the club, making a further 50 appearances before retiring from playing.

ABOVE Stamford the Lion entertains at the protected Stamford Bridge

Pitch Owners

CHELSEA PITCH OWNERS IS AN independent organisation that took out a substantial loan to purchase the freehold of the stadium and the name Chelsea FC. The purpose of CPO is to give fans the opportunity to buy a small number of shares in the company that owns the freehold of the pitch. This will ensure that if the developers ever looked to buy the land, regardless of how much it was worth, the shareholders could vote down any such motion.

The share capital of the company is not listed or traded on any stock exchange neither is there any intention to list the share capital of the company upon any investment exchange.

Therefore CPO shares do not increase or decrease in value. But it does help ensure that no one, now or in the future will develop the Bridge into anything other than one of the best stadiums in Europe in which to watch The Blues!

Player of the Year

OFFICIAL CHELSEA PLAYER OF THE YEAR LIST

1967	Peter Bonetti
1968	Charlie Cooke
1969	David Webb
1970	John Hollins
1971	John Hollins
1972	David Webb
1973	Peter Osgood
1974	Gary Locke

1975	Charlie Cooke
1976	Ray Wilkins
1977	Ray Wilkins
1978	Micky Droy
1979	Tommy Langley
1980	Clive Walker
1981	Petar Borota
1982	Mike Fillery
1983	Joey Jones
1984	Pat Nevin
1985	David Speedie

ABOVE LEFT 1988 Player of the Year Tony Dorigo

ABOVE RIGHT 1978 Player of the Year Micky Droy

BELOW LEFT 1974 Player of the Year Gary Locke

BELOW 1986 Player of the Year Eddie Niedzwiecki

PLAYER OF THE YEAR

1986	Eddie Niedzwiecki
1987	Pat Nevin
1988	Tony Dorigo
1989	Graham Roberts
1990	Ken Monkou
1991	Andy Townsend
1992	Paul Elliott
1993	Frank Sinclair
1994	Steve Clarke
1995	Erland Johnsen
1996	Ruud Gullit
1997	Mark Hughes
1998	Dennis Wise
1999	Gianfranco Zola
2000	Dennis Wise

RIGHT 1997 Player of the Year Mark Hughes

BELOW RIGHT 1992 Player of the Year Paul Elliott

BELOW 1991 Player of the Year Andy Townsend

2001	John Terry
2002	Carlo Cudicini
2003	Gianfranco Zola
2004	Frank Lampard
2005	John Terry
2006	John Terry
2007	Michael Essien

Quickest

THE EARLY GOAL ALL CHELSEA fans will remember came in the 1997 FA Cup Final when Chelsea beat Middlesbrough 2-0. While they were still taking their seats at Wembley or settling down in front of the telly, Italian midfielder Italian Roberto Di Matteo whacked a long-range shot past Boro's Ben Roberts to register the quickest goal in the fixture's long history. The official clock timed it at just 43 seconds.

But even champions can slip up as Chelsea did by letting Southampton's James Beattie's score the quickest goal of the Premiership season in 12 seconds for Southampton at the Bridge on 28 August 2004. Joe Cole was the culprit, conceding possession to set up the first goal conceded under Jose Mourinho. The strike was just two seconds slower than Ledley King's fastest ever Premiership goal in 2000.

Unfortunately for Beattie, he then deflected Eidur Gudjohnsen's backheader into his own net to cancel out the lead, and Chelsea eventually won 2-1 to ensure a four-game winning streak became five.

As if to show they hadn't learned their lesson, the Blues then went to the Millennium Stadium for the Carling (League) Cup Final in February 2005 and let Liverpool score the quickest goal in League Cup final history after just 45 seconds. But while John Arne Riise drew first blood with his thumping left-foot shot, Chelsea regained their composure to force extra time before goals by Drogba and Kezman ensured a 3-2 scoreline and the club's first trophy in five years. Moral: it ain't over till the fat lady sings!

ABOVE Roberto Di Matteo scores for Chelsea in the 1997 FA Cup Final

Ranieri

BORN IN ROME ON 20 OCTOBER 1951, Claudio spent his playing days with AS Roma, Catanzaro and Catania. At the end of his playing career he turned to coaching and then management, accepting his first managerial role with Campania.

After two years he moved on to Cagliari, taking the club into Serie A inside two years following successive promotions. His reputation enhanced, he then moved on to Napoli and subsequently Fiorentina in 1993.

It was at Fiorentina that he began to enjoy success, guiding the club to Italian Cup and Super Cup victories. Following this success he switched to Spain, taking over at Valencia and winning the Spanish Cup in 1998 and later guiding them into the Champions League for the first time. Claudio then accepted an offer to join Atletico Madrid, but wran-

gles with his chairman meant it was an uphill struggle and Atletico were relegated from the Spanish top flight.

After six months out of the game Claudio accepted an invitation to take over at Stamford Bridge in 2000, replacing the recently sacked Gianluca Vialli. His early days at Chelsea were also a struggle, with Vialli being very much a fans' favourite.

Claudio's stock wasn't helped by his inability to speak English, a situation not helped by the appointment of an interpreter who struggled with Italian and the printing of the manager's notes in the matchday programme in pidgin English!

Added to this was his constant changing of the team both before and during matches, with all three substitutions often taking place at once, which led many to question his tactical abilities. Slowly Claudio won everyone around, reaching the FA Cup final in 2002 and finding a way of

LEFT The Roman army General

BELOW Ranieri: Practise what you preach

ABOVE Ranieri speaks at a press conference

team coach was under threat and only the delivery of a major trophy would save his job.

Despite the mounting pressure Claudio retained his calm, winning over countless fans both inside and outside the club with the assured way he went about his business.

A stunning victory over Arsenal in the Champions League quarter-finals left him on the brink of delivering the greatest club prize of them all, but just as he had done at the beginning of his Chelsea career, he changed the side around at the wrong time.

From drawing away 1-1 against a Monaco side down to ten men, the second leg side lacked cohesion and leadership and slumped to a 3-1 defeat. It was too much of a mountain for the second half and Chelsea went out of the Champions League in the semi-final.

Claudio's chances of retaining his position went with them and in May 2004 it was confirmed that he was leaving the club.

Claudio subsequently returned to Valencia, helping them win the European Super Cup but lasted a single season in the job before leaving once again.

getting the best out of the players he had, especially as there wasn't any money to buy new ones at the start of the 2002-03 season.

He managed to qualify for the following season's Champions League and, with the arrival of Roman Abramovich, suddenly had almost unlimited funds available for team strengthening – he spent some £130 million during the course of the season.

As the months progressed speculation grew that Claudio's position as first

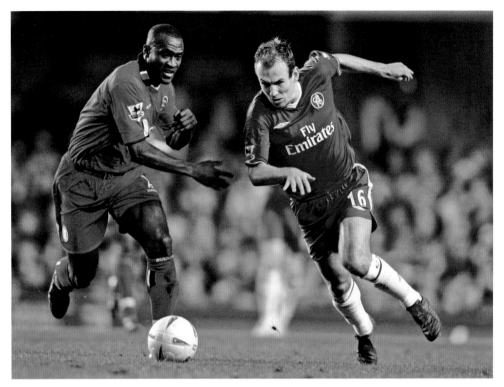

Robben

BORN IN BEDUM ON 23 JANUARY 198, Arjen has emerged as one of the brightest wing players in recent years.

After playing for his local club VV Bedum and then switched to Groningen where he made his League debut at the age of 16.

He was soon spotted by PSV Eindhoven Director of Football Frank Arnesen and a €4.2 million fee saw him transferred to the Dutch giants, although he was loaned back to Groningen for a year.

ABOVE Arjen Robben leaves another defender for dead

ROBBEN

When he arrived in Eindhoven his impact was almost immediate and he won his first cap for Holland in April 2003. In March 2004 he agreed to join Chelsea at the end of the season.

This was despite interest from Manchester United, among others, but as United were only prepared to offer

RIGHT Robben holds the Premiership trophy
BELOW SCORE!

€7 million, and with Chelsea offering much closer to PSV's valuation with €18 million, Chelsea landed their man. Unfortunately a dreadful injury sustained in a pre-season friendly meant Chelsea fans had to wait until October

before catching their first glimpse of the flying Dutchman, but just as before his impact was immediate.

He again suffered a bad injury midway through the season and there were fears he would miss the remainder of the season, but he returned in March 2005 as the season headed for a successful conclusion.

As vital for Holland as he could be for Chelsea, it is to be hoped that Arjen Robben enjoys a lengthy spell fit so that he can realise his vast potential.

Sexton

ABOVE The directors of Chelsea Football Club including film director Richard Attenborough (seated left) and Dave Sexton (standing right) with the FA Cup

BORN IN LONDON ON 6 APRIL 1930, Dave Sexton was the son of a middleweight boxer but chose football as his own profession, going on to play for Chelmsford City, Luton Town, West Ham United, Leyton Orient, Brighton & Hove Albion and Crystal Palace during his career, helping Brighton win the Third Division championship in 1958. At the end of his playing career Dave switched to coaching and established a good reputation at Chelsea, Fulham and Arsenal.

In 1965 he returned to Leyton Orient, this time as manager, and two years later returned to Stamford Bridge, replacing the recently departed Tommy Docherty. Whilst Dave inherited the nucleus of a good side, he bought wisely and constructed a side that could compete for the game's top honours, finally landing the FA Cup and European Cup Winners' Cup in successive seasons. He left Chelsea in 1974 and took over at QPR, where he was unfortunate not to win the League in 1976, later managing at Manchester United and Coventry.

Whilst that remains his last full time management role, Dave has been in demand for his coaching knowledge, assisting the England set up under Bobby Robson and later Sven Goran Eriksson, setting up a scouting network for the latter.

The first Technical Director of the FA National School at Lilleshall, Dave Sexton OBE still retains his affection for Chelsea, citing his FA Cup triumph of 1970 as the most memorable of his career.

For guiding Chelsea to the first sustained success in their history, Chelsea fans retain their affection for Dave Sexton too.

BELOW Chelsea manager Dave Sexton signs autographs for young fans

Shevchenko

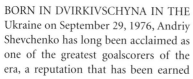

BORN IN DVIRKIVSCHYNA IN THE Ukraine on September 29, 1976, Andriy Shevchenko has long been acclaimed as one of the greatest goalscorers of the era, a reputation that has been earned with Dynamo Kiev, AC Milan and the Ukraine national side.

He began his career with Dynamo Kiev, making his debut during the 1993-94 season and going on to win the domestic League title five seasons in succession. His goalscoring exploits weren't only confined to Russia either, for he grabbed numerous goals in the UEFA Champions League and helped Dynamo Kiev reach the semi-finals in 1999 before being beaten by Bayern Munich.

Along with fellow Ukraine striker Sergei Rebrov, Andriy Shevchenko was the subject of numerous enquiries from Europe's top clubs, and whilst Rebrov moved on to Spurs for £11 million, Andriy preferred AC Milan and joined the club in the summer of 1999 for $26 million. He picked up a UEFA Champions League winners medal in 2003 and a runners-up medal in the same competition in 2005, the defeat by Liverpool going some way to convince Andriy that when it came time to move on, England and the Premier League would be the preferred option.

Rumours about a proposed move to Chelsea have been circulating for almost twelve months, with the club being reported to have offered £50 million and then £85 million for the most feared striker in the game. Whilst these offers were turned down by AC Milan and Andriy constantly expressed himself happy to remain in Italy, by the summer of 2006 the situation had changed and Andriy announced his intention to leave the club and began negotiations with Chelsea, finally agreeing a deal in May worth a reported £30 million. He has taken time to settle into the side, although he did pick up silverware in the shape of the Carling Cup. However, his season was brought to an early end by a hernia operation.

Sinclair

BORN IN LAMBETH on 3 December 1971, Frank began his Stamford Bridge career as a trainee and was upgraded to the professional ranks in 1989.

He made his League debut the following year and remained with the club for almost ten years, making 169 League appearances and scoring 7 goals (for Chelsea). He also had a spell on loan at West Bromwich during this period, making six appearances for the Baggies during the 1991-92 season.

A member of the side that won the FA Cup in 1997 he missed out on the Cup Winners Cup the following year and moved on to Leicester City during the summer of 1998.

He was to enjoy six seasons with the Foxes before moving on to Turf Moor and Burnley.

A Jamaican international with 24 full caps to his name, Frank had, prior to joining Leicester City, registered 11 goals for his then three clubs.

He is perhaps more famous for the number of own goals he has scored, all of which seem to be spectacular efforts that would have been worthy of being scored at the correct end!

LEFT Frank Sinclair celebrates scoring his goal against Real Betis

BELOW Sinclair-borne

Speedie

BORN IN GLENROTHES ON 20 February 1960, David was a much travelled but highly respected forward who gave great service to 11 clubs during the course of his career.

Signed as a junior by Barnsley he was promoted to the professional ranks in October 1978 and made a total of 23 appearances for the Yorkshire club, although he was unable to score.

He was sold to Darlington in June 1980 and, in a lower division, began to establish himself as a proven goalscorer, netting 21 goals in 88 appearances before being snapped up by Chelsea.

He arrived at Stamford Bridge in June 1982 and would ultimately form a lethal strike partnership with Kerry Dixon, who arrived a year later.

Over the course of five seasons David scored 47 goals in 162 appearances, but just as his partnership with Kerry was beginning to reap real dividends he was sold to an ambitious Coventry City and made his

debut for the club in the FA Charity Shield at Wembley.

He went on to make 122 appearances (netting 31 goals) for the Sky Blues before being surprisingly transferred to Liverpool in February 1991.

Playing in a more deep lying midfield position, David was unable to make a real impact at Anfield and was soon on his travels once again, joining Blackburn Rovers in August 1991. Nearly a year later he was sold to Southampton and later had spells at Birmingham City, West Bromwich Albion and West Ham United before finishing his career with Leicester City.

Stamford Bridge

STAMFORD BRIDGE IS SOMEWHAT unique among the major grounds, for whilst the likes of Old Trafford and Highbury were built to suit the needs of Manchester United and Arsenal respectively, Chelsea was formed to fill an existing ground!

The site that now houses Chelsea FC originally opening on 28 April 1877 as the home of the London Athletic Club and was used for athletics only.

In 1896 brothers HA (Gus) and JT Mears tried to buy the leasehold of the site, finally succeeding in 1904 following the death of the previous owner (a Mr Stunt) and the expiry of a clause in the original contract that gave the London Athletics Club two years grace after the death of the owner.

The Mears brothers finally got control of the site in September 1904 but even then were not convinced that a football club was the best way of filling the ground on a more regular basis. There was an exceptional offer on the table from the Great Western Railway Company that seemed closest to success

BELOW Chelsea playing at Stamford Bridge in 1919

(and would give the brothers a more than sizeable return on their investment) but tentative enquiries were made as to whether Fulham, the only other local side, would be interested in moving into Stamford Bridge, a plot that offered more potential than Craven Cottage.

Fulham turned them down, preferring to remain at the Cottage, which left only the prospect of Stamford Bridge becoming a coal dumping yard for the Great Western Railway.

Fate, or rather a dog, then took a hand; at a meeting with Gus Mears, friend Frederick Parker tried to convince Gus Mears that the ground could become a viable alternative to Crystal Palace, then the venue for the FA Cup final, which would realise a potential profit of £3,000 a game.

Mears was unconvinced until Mr Parker's dog bit him on the leg, and Gus Mears was so taken with the cool manner in which Mr Parker reacted, he reckoned he could trust his judgement on the fate of Stamford Bridge!

Whilst others set about building a side, Gus Mears and Frederick Parker concentrated on building a ground suitable. Impressed with what they saw in Glasgow, they employed architect Archibald Leitch to do the designs. His plan was simplicity itself, with a main stand (the East Stand) and banking around the other three sides to create a natural bowl.

It was originally intended that Stamford Bridge would accommodate

BELOW Stamford Bridge in 1969 covered in a blanket of snow

95,000 (most of them would have been without cover) but this figure was tested only once.

It was, however, the second biggest ground after Crystal Palace but it was not until after the First World War that Stamford Bridge got to host an FA Cup final, and then only for three years. Fears that Chelsea might reach the final and play on their own ground were heightened in 1920 when Chelsea made the semi-final, and by 1923 the FA had settled on a new and neutral venue for all future finals, Wembley Stadium. Stamford Bridge itself developed little until 1930 when the Shed End terrace and cover was erected, along with a greyhound track around the pitch!

For the next 40 or so years Stamford Bridge changed very little, although bits seemingly were added here and there and there was no real uniform design to the stadium.

That was to change in 1973 with the first phase in what was planned to be the construction of a new

Stamford Bridge, capable of accommodating 50,000 fans in an all-seater circular stadium.

The East Stand was the first to be built, an impressive three tier stand that towered over the rest of the ground, but the cost of building the stand virtually bankrupted the club and meant the rest of the plans remained unfulfilled.

With the club in such massive debt ownership of the ground passed out of their hands and there were fears for almost ten years that the club would have to consider moving elsewhere, but eventually ownership was won back in 1992 and two years later new and revised expansion plans were put into place.

The North Stand, built with funding from Matthew Harding and renamed in his honour following his death, was the first phase in a new circular style stadium, but this time the stands were nearer the pitch, generating a better atmosphere.

The Shed End was rebuilt in 1997, complete with the Chelsea Village Hotel, to generate additional income for the club, and in 1998 the final piece of the jigsaw, the West Stand, started. Problems over planning permission meant that the upper tier was not completed until three years later, but when finished lifted the capacity at Stamford Bridge to 42,449, all under cover.

The Chelsea Village complex also features two four star hotels, five restaurants, conference and banqueting facilities, a nightclub, health club and business centre.

Tambling

BORN IN STORRINGTON ON 18 September 1941, Bobby was spotted by Chelsea whilst playing for East Hampshire Schools and was taken on as an apprentice in July 1957 and upgraded to the professional ranks in September 1958.

He scored on his League debut for the club in February 1959 but it was to take the departure of Jimmy Greaves before Bobby was able to establish himself as a regular in the side.

Thereafter he was a prolific goalscorer, netting a Chelsea record of 164 League goals over the course of 302 appearances, including a record–equalling five in one match against Aston Villa in September 1966. A member of the side that won the League Cup in 1965 he also helped the club reach the FA Cup Final in 1967, netting Chelsea's goal in the 2-1 defeat by Spurs.

Unfortunately for Bobby, by the time Chelsea had re-assembled a side to challenge and win major honours his career at Stamford Bridge had started to falter, hampered by injuries and he was loaned to Crystal Palace in January 1970.

The move became permanent during the summer, with Palace paying £40,000 to secure his services, and over the next three years Bobby made 68 League appearances and scored 12 goals. He wound down his playing career in Ireland, having spells with Cork Celtic (where he also served as a player-manager), Waterford and Shamrock Rovers before finally retiring.

Capped for England at schoolboy and Under 23 level, Bobby also won three full caps, netting one goal.

ABOVE Tambling tries a shot

BELOW Bobby dazzler!

Terry

BORN IN BARKING ON 7 December 1980, 'JT' came through Chelsea's youth ranks, representing the club at youth and reserve level before being handed his first team debut in October 1998.

A total of just six League appearances in two seasons prompted speculation that John might be better served trying his luck elsewhere and he had a spell on loan at Nottingham Forest but in the 2000-01 season John began to break into the side on a more regular basis.

The following season he had made the central defensive position largely his own, prompting calls for him to be included in the England World Cup squad for 2002 but an incident outside a nightclub led to him being charged with affray and banned from being selected for any England side until the matter was settled.

RIGHT 'JT'

OPPOSITE RIGHT TOP Yet another Terry tackle

OPPOSITE RIGHT BOTTOM John Terry lifts the Premiership trophy again in 2006

He was subsequently cleared on all charges in August 2002. Over the next three years John Terry let his football do the talking, breaking into the fringes of the England side, initially as an obvious replacement for Rio Ferdinand or Sol Campbell but, for the last 12 months or so, as a first choice player himself, with Rio and Sol having to battle for the other slot. First handed the captain's armband at Chelsea during the 2003-04 season whenever Marcel Desailly was out of the side, John has since made the role his own and therefore collected the League Cup and FA Premiership in 2005 and the Premier trophy again in 2006.

Largely seen as the rock upon which Chelsea built their championship winning side he superbly marshalled the defence throughout the season, conceding only 15 goals and also weighed in with one or two vital strikes at the other end.

His contribution to the club during the season was appreciated not only inside Stamford Bridge

(Jose Mourinho dubbed him "the best centre-back in the world") but also outside as he collected the Player of the Year award from the PFA. Chelsea's defence of the Premiership faltered during 2006-07, due in large part to the enforced absence of John Terry through a recurring back problem. A normally miserly Chelsea defence leaked extra goals during his absence, proof of his worth to the team.

The Trophy Cabinet

RIGHT Chelsea celebrate winning the FA Premier League once again in 2006

Trophy	Years
League Title	1955, 2005, 2006
FA Cup	1970, 1997, 2000, 2007
Cup Winners Cup	1971, 1998
Super Cup	1998
Community Shield	1955, 2000, 2005
FA Cup Runners-Up	1915, 1967, 1994, 2002
FA Cup Semi-Finalists	1911, 1920, 1932, 1950, 1952, 1965, 1966, 1996
Champions League Semi-Finalists	2004, 2005, 2007
League Cup Winners	1965, 1998, 2005, 2007
League Cup Runners-Up	1972
Charity Shield Runners-Up	1970, 1997
Old League Division Two Winners (now called 'The Championship')	1984, 1989
Full Members/ZDS Cup Winners	1986, 1990
FA Youth Cup Winners	1960, 1961
FA Youth Cup Runners-Up	1958

Three Hundred Club

Player	Dates played	Apps	Goals	Apps with subs
Ron Harris	(1961-80)	795	14	784+11
Peter Bonetti	(1959-79)	729	–	729
John Hollins	(1963-75) & (1983-84)	592	64	592
Dennis Wise	(1990-2001)	445	76	434+11
Steve Clarke	(1987-98)	421	10	407+1
Eddie McCreadie	(1962-74)	410	5	405+5
John Bumstead	(1976-91)	409	44	379+30
Ken Armstrong	(1946-57)	402	30	402
Peter Osgood	(1964-74) & (1978-79)	380	150	376+4
Charlie Cooke	(1966-72) & (1974-78)	373	30	360+13

LEFT The 1972-3 Chelsea FC squad, featuring goalkeeper Peter Bonetti (back row, fourth from left) and captain Ron Harris, who have made the most and second most appearances for Chelsea

THREE HUNDRED CLUB

Player	Dates played	Apps	Goals	Apps with subs
George Smith	(1921-32)	370	–	370
Bobby Tambling	(1958-70)	370	202	366+4
Haroid Miller	(1923-39)	363	44	363
Frank Blunstone	(1953-64)	347	54	347
Marvin Hinton	(1963-76)	344	4	328+16
Peter Houseman	(1962-75)	343	39	325+18
Tommy Law	(1925-39)	319	19	319
Gary Locke	(1972-82)	317	4	315+2
Micky Droy	(1970-85)	313	19	302+11
Graeme Le Saux	(1987-93) & (1997-03)	312	16	280+32
Gianfranco Zola	(1996-2003)	312	80	260+52
Jackie Crawford	(1923-34)	308	27	308
Bobby McNeil	(1914-27)	307	32	307
Frank Lampard	(2001-)	328	50	309+19

RIGHT Tommy Law (right) shakes hands with Sam Weaver. Tommy made 319 appearances for Chelsea

Gianluca was immediately offered the position of player-manager.

The following month he led the club to victory in the Coca Cola League Cup

Hav... players since his a... of dressing room unrest w... thing the club needed and in Septe... 2000 he was sacked.

He eventually resurfaced as manager of Watford, but without the same kind of resources his tenure did not last long and he has since appeared on television as a pundit. Despite the circumstances surrounding his removal, Gianluca presided over a time of sustained success, something the club had been striving for for decades.

Under-rated

BELOW Scott Parker battles with Steed Malbranque of Fulham

PLAYING UNDER THE MEDIA spotlight in Chelsea's current team means that few players can consider themselves underrated. Claude Makelele was not one of the world-famous 'Galacticos' at Real Madrid, but since his arrival at Stamford Bridge has become one of the most respected defensive midfielders in the game.

The Chelsea player most underrated in the Championship season of 2004-05 was undoubtedly injury-hit Scott Parker, who never got a first-team chance after his transfer from Charlton. Hopefully he will not come back to haunt Chelsea in the colours of new club Newcastle United.

Players of the past who tended to be overlooked by the press (if not the fans) in favour of their superstar team-mates include Peter Houseman, a left winger/midfielder who laid on goals for the likes of Osgood and Hutchinson in the late 1960s/early 1970s, and whole-hearted Welsh defender Joey Jones who starred in the early 1980s.

More recently who can forget the 2004 heroics of fourth-choice goalkeeper Marco Ambrosio as Chelsea left Highbury with a 2-1 Champions League victory. Wayne Bridge wrote the headlines with the deciding goal four minutes from time, but it was the underrated keeper's heroics that ensured the home team

OPPOSITE RIGHT Gianluca Vialli in action

RIGHT Marco Ambrosio

BELOW Dave Beasant

were restricted to a single goal. And talking of keepers, Dave Beasant was shipped out by Ian Porterfield when he suffered a 'mare' against Norwich in 1992 – yet would continue to play professionally into his mid forties. His manager, by contrast, failed to see out the season...

In terms of underrated Chelsea teams, one candidate is John Neal's mid-1980s side which included the likes of Kerry Dixon, Pat Nevin and Mickey Thomas. But after 2005's glorious campaign, Chelsea are unlikely ever to be under-rated again!

...to Serie A

...time he came to England in ...6, he had also played for Juventus and won every domestic and European honour available, including two Serie A titles (one for each club), four Italian Cups, the UEFA Cup, the European Cup Winners' Cup and the UEFA Champions League, captaining Juventus in the 1996 final.

A few days later a free transfer saw him join the growing foreign revolution at Stamford Bridge and join compatriot

Under-rated

PLAYING UNDER THE MEDIA spotlight in Chelsea's current team means that few players can consider themselves underrated. Claude Makelele was not one of the world-famous 'Galacticos' at Real Madrid, but since his arrival at Stamford Bridge has become one of the most respected defensive midfielders in the game.

The Chelsea player most underrated in the Championship season of 2004-05 was undoubtedly injury-hit Scott Parker, who never got a first-team chance after his transfer from Charlton. Hopefully he will not come back to haunt Chelsea in the colours of new club Newcastle United.

Players of the past who tended to be overlooked by the press (if not the fans) in favour of their superstar team-mates include Peter Houseman, a left winger/midfielder who laid on goals for

BELOW Scott Parker battles with Steed Malbranque of Fulham

UNDER-RATED

the likes of Osgood and Hutchinson in the late 1960s/early 1970s, and whole-hearted Welsh defender Joey Jones who starred in the early 1980s.

More recently who can forget the 2004 heroics of fourth-choice goalkeeper Marco Ambrosio as Chelsea left Highbury with a 2-1 Champions League victory. Wayne Bridge wrote the headlines with the deciding goal four minutes from time, but it was the underrated keeper's heroics that ensured the home team were restricted to a single goal. And talking of keepers, Dave Beasant was shipped out by Ian Porterfield when he suffered a 'mare' against Norwich in 1992 – yet would continue to play professionally into his mid forties. His manager, by contrast, failed to see out the season...

In terms of underrated Chelsea teams, one candidate is John Neal's mid-1980s side which included the likes of Kerry Dixon, Pat Nevin and Mickey Thomas. But after 2005's glorious campaign, Chelsea are unlikely ever to be under-rated again!

OPPOSITE RIGHT Gianluca Vialli in action

RIGHT Marco Ambrosio

BELOW Dave Beasant

Vialli

BORN IN CREMONA ON 9 JULY 1964, Gianluca Vialli is one of only a handful of men to have both played for and managed Chelsea, combining both positions for a period towards the end of the 1990s.

He began his career with the local Cremonese club and made just over 100 appearances before a switch to Serie A with Sampdoria.

By the time he came to England in 1996, he had also played for Juventus and won every domestic and European honour available, including two Serie A titles (one for each club), four Italian Cups, the UEFA Cup, the European Cup Winners' Cup and the UEFA Champions League, captaining Juventus in the 1996 final.

A few days later a free transfer saw him join the growing foreign revolution at Stamford Bridge and join compatriot

VIALLI

Gianfranco Zola. His impact was immediate, finishing the 1996-97 season as Chelsea's top goalscorer and had collected a winners medal in the FA Cup (he replaced Gianfranco Zola some 12 minutes before the end of the match).

However, Gianluca's greater contribution was being felt in the dressing room, and when Ruud Gullit was sensationally sacked in February 1998,

(although he didn't play) and two months after that victory in the European Cup Winners' Cup (in which he did). In May 2000 came further glories in the FA Cup, but it was to be something of a swansong for Gianluca.

Having spent some £57 million on players since his appointment, rumours of dressing room unrest were the last thing the club needed and in September 2000 he was sacked.

He eventually resurfaced as manager of Watford, but without the same kind of resources his tenure did not last long and he has since appeared on television as a pundit. Despite the circumstances surrounding his removal, Gianluca presided over a time of sustained success, something the club had been striving for for decades.

Gianluca was immediately offered the position of player-manager.

The following month he led the club to victory in the Coca Cola League Cup

Walker

BORN IN OXFORD ON 26 MAY 1957, Clive joined Chelsea as an apprentice and moved up to the professional ranks in April 1975.

It took him a couple of years to make a regular breakthrough into the side but when called upon he usually turned in dazzling performances, none more so than in 1977 when Chelsea beat Liverpool, then reigning European champions 4-2 in an FA Cup tie at Stamford Bridge, with Clive contributing two of the goals. Although he made 224 appearances for the club in his nine years, he struggled to shake off the tag of super-sub, even though the facts were somewhat different; he only made 33 appearances as a substitute.

However, as his introduction from the bench usually coincided with an upturn in Chelsea's performance, perhaps it was a moniker well earned.

Clive left Chelsea in July 1984 with their First Division status being reclaimed and having netted 60 League goals during his time at Stamford Bridge, and would later give equally good service to Queens Park Rangers,

BELOW
Walker of Chelsea goes in for a tackle against Ossie Ardiles of Spurs

Fulham and Brighton where he finished his playing career. He later became a television pundit.

Webb

BORN IN STRATFORD ON 9 APRIL 1946, David was an amateur with West Ham United before moving to Leyton Orient to begin his professional career. He spent nearly three years with the club before moving to the South coast to join Southampton and over the next two years developed into one of the best full backs in the country.

Chelsea signed him in February 1968 and over the course of the next six years he became a vital member of the side. David's Chelsea career is perhaps best summed up by two matches against the same opposition, Leeds United in the FA Cup final of 1970. In the first match, playing a strict full back role he was given a torrid time by Eddie Gray, being constantly beaten by the trickery of the Scottish winger.

At the end of the match, which finished a 2-2 draw, both Chelsea in general and David in particular looked as though they had achieved an unlikely reprieve. In the second match manager Dave Sexton switched things around, handling responsibility for marking Gray to Ron Harris and moving David

into a more central defensive role.

Whilst Gray's threat was blunted by Harris, David thrived on the space and freedom he now had and in extra time it was he who headed in the winning goal.

The following season he was an equally vital member of the side that won the European Cup Winners' Cup against Real Madrid.

He proved his versatility to Chelsea in December 1971 when, with Peter Bonetti, John Phillips and Steve Sherwood all injured, he played against Ipswich Town in goal! Remarkably, after dropping to his knees and praying in front of the Shed, he helped the Blues keep a clean sheet in a 2-0 victory! David remained at Stamford Bridge until July 1974 when he left to join Queens Park Rangers, subsequently playing for Leicester City, Derby

County, Bournemouth and Torquay United before retiring as a player in 1984.

He then became manager of Torquay and also had three spells in charge at Southend United. He was also briefly manager at Stamford Bridge, answering a crisis call from the club in 1993 with a brief to conduct an audit of the playing staff during his spell in charge.

It was widely believed that David would benefit from the audit but, although he did a good job in his few months in charge, Glenn Hoddle was subsequently lured from Swindon to take over control.

ABOVE Webb fights for the high ball

LEFT David Webb clears the danger

Wilkins

BORN IN HILLINGDON ON 14 September 1956, Ray Wilkins enjoyed a long and illustrious career as a player and has proved to be a more than capable coach and pundit since he officially retired.

Nicknamed Butch during his childhood, he joined Chelsea as an apprentice and rose through the ranks to make his debut against Norwich City in October 1973.

It was the 1974-75 season that saw him become established as a permanent fixture in Chelsea's midfield, progressing to become captain of the side at just 19 years of age, the youngest captain in the club's history. This was despite the presence of several older, more experienced players on the club's books; Ray's ability to appear calm and composed when all around him was mayhem (such was the nature of

BELOW Ray Wilkins watches from the dugout

Chelsea's play at this period) was an inspiration to his teammates.

It was also said that his play showed a certain negativity, with Ray often playing the square sideways pass rather than looking forward earning him the addi-

tional nickname of The Crab. Despite suffering relegation under his captaincy Chelsea bounced back and Ray Wilkins' reputation soared with it, culminating in an £800,000 transfer to Manchester United in August 1979.

Ray was with United for five years, helping them win the 1983 FA Cup (his only domestic honour) before a move to AC Milan for £1.5 million in 1984 where he found his true vocation. First capped for England in 1976 against Italy, Ray won 84 caps over the next ten years, captaining his country on ten occasions and scoring three goals.

ABOVE Ray Wilkins with Graham Rix

LEFT Brothers Graham (left) and Ray ('Butch') Wilkins

Wise

BORN IN LONDON ON 16 December 1966, Dennis joined Southampton as an apprentice straight from school but never made the grade at The Dell, being allowed to leave and subsequently joining Wimbledon in March 1985.

He made his debut for The Dons before the season was out but made just four appearances during the 1985-86 season. The following season, Wimbledon's first in the First Division, saw Dennis become something of a regular and the heart, along with Vinnie Jones, of the so-called Crazy Gang.

Dennis was an integral part of the side that won the FA Cup in 1987-88, netting the winner in the semi-final and responsible for crossing the ball over for the only goal of the final.

One of the last of the original Crazy Gang left, Dennis moved on to Chelsea in July 1990 for £1.6 million.

Over the course of the next ten years he gave Chelsea exceptional service, both on and off the pitch, and was the heartbeat and captain of the side that won two FA Cups and the European Cup Winners' Cup.

The higher profile he enjoyed at Chelsea was rewarded with his first cap for England in 1991 and he would go on to win 12 caps for his country, scoring one goal.

In June 2001, after 332 League appearances and 113 games in other

end of the 2004-05 season he resigned and returned to Southampton, where his career began. In May 2006 he was named player-manager of Swindon Town, with former Chelsea legend Gus Poyet his assistant.

Aside from his efforts on the pitch on behalf of the club, Chelsea fans have good reason to honour Dennis, for along with Ken Bates he galvanised the club as part of the Chelsea Owners club, ultimately ensuring the club's future at Stamford Bridge.

He is still fondly remembered in song by fans on most match days for his "******* great goal in the San Siro" equalising in the 1-1 draw with AC Milan on October 26 1999.

competitions (he is fourth in the all-time list of Chelsea appearances), Dennis was allowed to join Leicester City, linking him once again with his former mentor Dave Bassett, but during the summer of 2002, an altercation with a teammate saw him sacked by the club and he subsequently joined Millwall. Later elevated to player-manager, he guided them to their first FA Cup final (Dennis's fifth) in 2004, but at the

BELOW Jon Harley, Dennis Wise, and John Terry help launch the new Chelsea kit in 2001

Wright-Phillips

BORN IN LONDON ON 25 October 1981, the stepson of former Arsenal and England striker Ian Wright, Shaun began his career as a trainee at Nottingham Forest.

He was surprisingly released by the club, who claimed he was too fragile to withstand the physical side of the game, Shaun joined Manchester City and set about proving his detractors wrong.

Used more as an old-style winger to supply the front men, Shaun is also able to cut inside and score goals on his own, a style that soon had him being linked with a call-up to the full England side. He made his full debut against the Ukraine in August 2004 and scored after a jinking run, a goal that added to his already growing list of admirers.

As the 2004-05 season came to a close so did speculation as to his future with Manchester City, with a host of clubs lining up offers. Although he was widely expected to join Arsenal, where his step-father had enjoyed a successful career, the only club who came close to matching Manchester City's £22 million valuation was Chelsea, who offered £21 million.

Whilst he struggled to establish himself in the side during his first season at Stamford Bridge, he did help win the Premiership even if it was at the expense of his place in the England set up. The following season he became more of a regular, collecting a winner's medal from the Carling Cup and re-establishing himself in the England squad.

X-tra time

Whilst Chelsea have featured in many matches that have gone into extra time, perhaps the most vital were in the FA Cup finals of 1970.

The first match at Wembley, on a heavy and energy sapping pitch, had seen Chelsea constantly playing catch-up against Leeds United, equalising for a second time shortly before the end of the allocated 90 minutes.

Extra time was little more than an exercise in survival for both sides, as cramp and strains began to affect the twenty two players out on the pitch.

The replay at Old Trafford seemed set to continue in a similar fashion, with Leeds taking the lead and being pegged back by Peter Osgood's diving header.

This time, however, Chelsea showed the more determination during extra time, creating a number of chances that might have put the match beyond doubt.

As it was, Ian Hutchinson's long throw was flicked on at the near post and David Webb stole in at the back to head home the decisive winner.

Lifting the FA Cup enabled the club to assume the mantle of Kings of the King's Road and was followed a year later by winning the European Cup Winners' Cup, and it owed everything to two completely different performances during extra time.

Youth Team

THE CHELSEA OF 2005 MAY WELL have been saddled with a reputation of a club that is prepared to buy the finished article with regard to players for any position within the team. Fifty years ago the focus at Stamford Bridge was very much on youth.

Although manager Ted Drake had managed to guide the club to their first League Championship, it was with a side that had a high average age. Recognising that the future would need younger, perhaps even fitter players, Ted Drake scoured the capital and beyond for the best schoolboy talent that was available.

One or two players, seemingly destined for other clubs, such as Jimmy Greaves, believed to be on the verge of signing for Spurs, were encouraged to make their way to Stamford Bridge and sign for Chelsea.

The youth team thus began to feature players who would later become first team regulars, earning the club the moniker of Drake's Ducklings and began to emerge as potential rivals to their foes in the north.

Chelsea made the final of the FA Youth Cup for the first time in 1958, losing narrowly 7-6 on aggregate, but two years later, in 1961, the cup was lifted for the first time with an emphatic 5-2 aggregate victory over Preston.

The cup remained at Stamford Bridge 12 months later too, this time Everton being seen off 5-3. Whilst Chelsea have not been to the final since, there has still an impressive youth set-up at the club, as the emergence of Ray Wilkins, John Terry and countless others would confirm.

Zola

BORN IN OLIENA, SARDINIA ON 5 July 1966, Gianfranco Zola remains the most popular and amongst the most successful of all Chelsea's overseas recruits.

He began his career with the Sardinian club Nuorese in 1984 and later with Torres, finally being spotted and signing for Serie A club Napoli in 1989.

Initially used as something of an understudy to Diego Maradona, Gianfranco helped Napoli win the Italian title in 1990.

The following year he picked up a winners medal in the Italian Super Cup and collected the first of his 35 caps for Italy after being selected by coach Arrigo Sacchi.

In 1993 he moved on to Parma AC and two years later helped them win the UEFA Cup (2-1 on aggregate against fellow Italian club Juventus), the Italian Cup and finish runners-up in Serie A, they're highest ever placing.

ABOVE Gianfranco Zola celebrates scoring

In November 1996 a £4.5 million fee brought him to Stamford Bridge and had an immediate effect on the club; at the end of the season they had won the FA Cup and Gianfranco had been named Footballer of the Year by the Football Writers' Association, perhaps the only winner to have received the accolade without completing an entire season.

There was better to follow, for the following season Chelsea won the Coca Cola League Cup and European Cup Winners' Cup, with Gianfranco scoring the only goal of the game against fb Stuttgart.

Further success came in the European Super Cup in 1998 and the FA Cup in 2000, the last at the old Wembley. One of Chelsea's favourite sons finally moved on in 2003, returning home to join Cagliari Calcio and helping them return to Serie A.

Such is the affection he is held at Stamford Bridge, however, that he was voted the best ever Chelsea player by the fans.

RIGHT Zola in action

BELOW Gianfranco Zola shows off his OBE for his services to football

In November 2004, he was given an honorary OBE (Order of the British Empire) in a special ceremony in Rome.

ABOVE Author Jules Gammond with his hero Joe Cole

The pictures in this book were provided courtesy of the following:

GETTY IMAGES
101 Bayham Street, London NW1 0AG

PA PHOTOS
www.paphotos.com

Design and artwork by Kevin Gardner

Published by Green Umbrella Publishing

Publishers Jules Gammond and Vanessa Gardner

Written by Graham Betts and Jules Gammond with Michael Heatley

In Memory of life-long Blues fan Mo Claridge
31st March 1951 – 25th December 2005